**Nancy Belfer** is a textile artist and teacher at the State University College at Buffalo. Her work has been shown in numerous regional and national exhibitions, including *Craftsmen of the Eastern States* and *Stitching* at the museum of Contemporary Crafts in New York, and *Objects U.S.A.*, the collection of American crafts compiled by the Johnson Wax Company. An M.F.A. graduate of the School for American Craftsmen, she has been working in the areas of weaving, stitching, and batik.

# Designing in Stitching and Appliqué

NANCY BELFER

A SPECTRUM BOOK

PRENTICE-HALL, INC., Englewood Cliffs, New Jersey 07632

*Library of Congress Cataloging in Publication Data*

Belfer, Nancy.
    Designing in stitching and appliqué.

    (The Creative handcrafts series)    (A Spectrum Book)
    Bibliography: p.
    1. Needlework.    2. Appliqué.    I. Title.
TT750.B45    1977        746.4'4        76-57240
ISBN 0-13-202010-6

Frontispiece: *Fragmented Journey* (55" x 36" x 3") (author)

Prentice-Hall International, Inc., *London*
Prentice-Hall of Australia Pty. Limited, *Sydney*
Prentice-Hall of Canada, Ltd., *Toronto*
Prentice-Hall of India Private Limited, *New Delhi*
Prentice-Hall of Japan, Inc., *Tokyo*
Prentice-Hall of Southeast Asia Pte. Ltd., *Singapore*
Whitehall Books Limited, *Wellington, New Zealand*

# Contents

# Acknowledgments

Many of my students, colleagues and friends helped immeasurably in the preparation of this book. Their kindness and cooperation are greatly appreciated.

Folk art and historic textiles were loaned from personal collections by Dr. Anna P. Burrell (Indian crewel rug, page 7); Winifred Hanny (American patchwork quilt, page 12); Suzanne Katz (San Blas molas, page 4, 43; embroidered cloth, page 10); Melvin Morris, A.I.A. (applique wall textile from Yugoslavia, color insert); and Randi Stevelman (Indian head cloth, page 8).

Thanks are due, also, to Larry Salmon, Curator of Textiles, Museum of Fine Arts, Boston; Mrs. John Arnold of the Canadian Handcraft Guild; the Textile Arts Club of the Cleveland Museum of Art; and James Stewart Polshek and Associates, Architects.

Numerous textile artists graciously responded to my requests for samples of their work, and my students were consistently generous in their willingness to contribute. They are credited by caption.

The black and white photography was done by Paul Pasquarello, with rare competence and dedication to quality. Drawings of basic stitches are from CREATIVE USE OF STITCHES by Vera P. Guild, published by Davis Publications, Inc., Worcester, MA.

# 1 Introduction

This book is for anyone who has responded to the richly varied appeal of yarns, threads, and cloth—the medium of fibers. It is an introduction to the many ways these materials can be used expressively and an invitation to begin a journey leading toward personal creative involvement.

In recent years, artists in textiles have demonstrated a boldness of vision that reflects the innovative thinking in all areas of fine arts. Ancient techniques are used in new and daring ways; different materials are combined with great flair and inventiveness. In addition, more and more people who have never thought of themselves as artists are becoming aware of the many opportunities for working directly with these inviting and challenging materials.

For the beginner, ways are shown to gain confidence in handling the materials and using the techniques effectively when evolving designs. Improvisation is encouraged, but along with this, an ever-sharpening sense of critical discernment gradually develops. In yarns and cloth, there are numerous variations in color, weight, and textural surface; these qualities are inspiring in themselves. There is

1

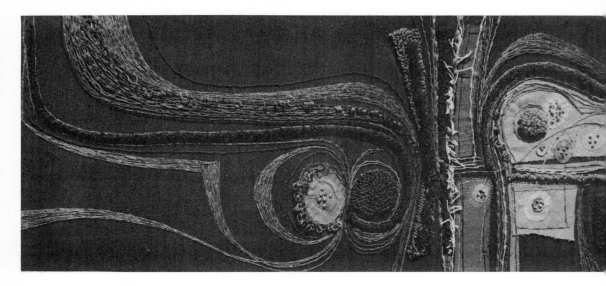

**Figure 1.1**  *Bright Harvest*   (16″ x 48″), by the author. On a background of olive-brown wool, stitching, appliqué, and hooking are combined.

no need to foster a dependence on "how-to-do-it" directions which usually result in clichés of simple "prettiness." This is an approach that negates many of the real values of art activity. It is more important for the beginner to learn by making personal discoveries and thus realize his own potential, find his own direction.

Basic technical information is presented for the various methods discussed. These techniques should be understood, but always with the realization that such skills are but one aspect of the work and should not restrict or inhibit designing. All methods of working are open to new ideas, new experimentation.

More experienced artists will find stimulating examples of work in a wide range of expression which will hopefully suggest fresh directions as well as unique ways of using the materials. In the careful study of what others have accomplished, we can enlarge our own vision of what is possible.

To those whose interest is in collecting or appreciating the many facets of work in this medium, the varied illustrations present a compact gallery. These offer a fascinating array of work in stitching and appliqué processes, along with related techniques in relief and sculptural forms in cloth.

**Figure 1.2**    In this woven wall hanging by Nancy Dayton, areas of stitching and macramé knotting are effectively included.

**Figure 1.3** Mola design in appliqué cutwork by Indians of the San Blas Islands.

# 2 Past and Present

Stitching and appliqué work are among the most ancient arts, and the needle was certainly a worthy tool for early man. This simple device made many things possible, especially the seaming together of smaller pieces of skins or matting into larger and more useful garments and covers. Most primitive societies, widely scattered geographically as well as in time, evolved the concept of the needle as a slender, sharp tool which could pierce through a prestructured fabric, drawing other material into it. In addition to its purely functional application, there was the opportunity, too tempting to ignore, of adding some extra stitches as a decoration.

From the many fragments that have been found, there is little doubt that the structuring and embellishment of fabric with surface motifs and patterns are activities that have origins going back to the earliest history of humankind. Beginning with the most basic seaming of utilitarian garments, skills slowly developed that seemed to parallel an instinctive need for ornamentation. Certain patterns and figures eventually were thought to have magical powers and were carefully worked on ceremonial cloths used in ritual worship services. Com-

**Figure 2.1**   Detail of mantle, wool embroidery on wool, Peru, Paracas culture, 500-300 B.C. (courtesy, Museum of Fine Arts, Boston). Closely worked stitching fills the symbolic figure, a creature of human, animal, and serpent parts.

plex arrangements of symbolic motifs decorated the cloaks and tunics of those who were powerful and wealthy.

Images and patterns reflecting the attitudes and beliefs of many cultures are evident in the textile fragments of the past, some simple and almost childlike, others with a complexity that is astonishing. Where no actual examples exist, writings, paintings, and statuary give evidence of hand-embellished garments and hangings. Even a very brief review of the numerous types of stitching and appliqué work of past centuries shows how these arts were adapted to fit the particular needs of each culture.

Needlework of elaborate refinement was done in both the Near and Far East. In China, especially, there is a textile tradition possibly going back to 3000 B.C. Intricate embroideries were very much a part of religious and community life and personal garments, also, were decorated with great skill. Both China and Japan greatly valued these arts, the essential character of the images remaining unchanged for centuries.

The peoples of India, too, produced beautiful embroidery work for thousands of years. The Indians were masterful in all of the textile arts, weaving, dyeing, and printing and the various stitching techniques. Large hangings, ornamented with precious stones, mirrors, and metallic threads were made for the palaces and temples; but along with this, a very strong folk art tradition always existed, so that on a lesser scale, these arts flourished among all the people.

From the earliest development of Western civilization, the textile arts were prevalent to some degree. The wall murals of Egyptian tombs picture needlework ornamentation on garments in several techniques. There are references to stitching in the Bible and in Homeric writings. Through wars, travel, and trade, the ancient world came to know and cherish hand-decorated cloth. Alexander was impressed with the embroidered tent of Darius and ordered one made for himself. Later, the Romans imported numerous embroidered hangings from the Near East.

**Figure 2.2**    An Indian rug from Kashmir, the background cloth completely filled with chain stitching in fine worsted wool, forming an arrangement of leaves, jungle birds, and animals.

**Figure 2.4** A bride's head cloth from India embroidered in yellow and red, with small round mirrors set around the border.

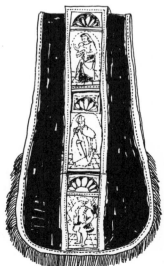

**Figure 2.3** An old crewel pattern, typical of the designs brought to England from India during the eighteenth century, was adapted in hooking by Elva Hasselfeldt for this bellpull.

**Figure 2.5** Back of linen chasuble, embroidered with silk. Flanders. 16th century.

With the growth of Christianity, these arts, like all others, served the Church and conveyed its message to those who could not read. In hundreds of altar cloths and wall hangings, elaborate images of Byzantine influence were worked with meticulous skill. Ecclesiastical garments, as well, were richly decorated with embroidery stitches.

Of the few preserved pieces of secular embroidery from the eleventh century, the Bayeux Tapestry is outstanding. Twenty inches high and two hundred and seventy feet long, it records in episodic or cartoonlike manner the historical events relating to the Battle of Hastings. The design has enormous vitality and the hand-embroidered figures form a catalog of information about battle dress, shields, weapons, even ships and horses. Stitched in wool on a linen background, this work has been called, by some scholars, coarse and crudely executed when compared to the more refined standard applied to the religious work of the same period.

In the centuries that followed, political and religious events affected western Europe in many ways, the arts included. With the Crusades, the medieval warriors returned with their spoils: precious trophies, banners, and costumes glowing with magnificent work in stitching and appliqué. This profusion of rich materials set with jewels and precious stones was to set new fashions among the aristocracy. In the French and English courts, men's coats and women's dresses became so costly because of their elaborate decoration that laws were passed to limit the sumptuousness of the styles.

This laborious work was done by hired women and apprenticed young girls. The stitches were very fine and the standards were very high; there are records of a set of church vestments taking twenty-six years for completion. This was not uncommon. For hundreds of

**Figure 2.6**  Embroidered glove. England, 17th century.

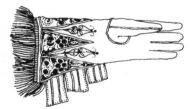

**Figure 2.7**  Embroidered wedding dress, cotton and linen. Palestine, about 1920.

**Figure 2.8**    A small cloth coverlet, embroidered with floral motifs and decorated with braid and fringe. Peasant art from eastern Europe.

years, the textile arts of western Europe seemed to reflect only the needs of those of wealth and power.

A different attitude motivated the embroidery work of central and eastern Europe. Here is a true people's art full of color and vitality. Folk traditions and national costumes emphasized a gay profusion of embroidered motifs executed in meticulous craftsmanship. These costumes (for both men and women), shawls, hats, and capes were decorated out of a love of "doing" that was reflected in the pride of wearing. In addition to garments, all manner of household articles were embroidered: curtains, bedspreads, pillow coverings, and household linens. These were things to be treasured but also to be used and perhaps passed on to the next generation.

On the American continent, all of the Indian cultures were familiar with some form of stitching and appliqué work. Outstanding among these is the textile work of the Peruvians. Their accomplishments in weaving are held in very special esteem, but in the Paracas and Nazca areas, impressive woven textiles embellished with embroidery stitches have been found. The beautifully worked mantles, ponchos, and ceremonial cloths show a superb knowledge of both weaving and embroidery. The motifs relate to religious symbolism, demon-creatures, snakes, and stylized bird, animal, and human forms.

Later, and under very different circumstances, the early American settlers in colonial times gave new interpretation to many kinds of traditional European needlework. The numerous quilts produced in appliqué and patchwork methods form a gracious heritage that is being revived with new interest today. In the colonial quilts preserved in many historical museums, the lively pattern effects and geometric arrangements are examined now with a renewed awareness of their crisp, mosaiclike shapes and complex optical designs.

The Victorian influence resulted in an unbelievable profusion of needlework, almost a mania, with stitches decorating just about every available space on wearing apparel and household articles. The designing was not strong, relying for the most part on the continual repetition of long-used floral patterns. This was also a time of emerging technology, when older ways of working no longer seemed significant. After the invention of the Jacquard loom, cloth could be woven mechanically with very complex color and pattern changes. The Schiffli embroidery machine, coming into use in mid-nineteenth century, could rapidly produce hundreds of stitch variations, commercially duplicating hand embroidery work.

Working in this medium today places great emphasis on expressive values. We can look back at work done in the past and marvel at the intricate workmanship or complexity of design, remembering that these pieces were useful and relevant for their own time. They cannot be models for us to imitate, but provide instead a way of understanding and appreciating how others have used these materials for their own purposes.

Even a very brief review of some of the needlework of the past shows that each culture used these arts for its own needs, sometimes conforming to traditions that have continued for many generations. Stitching and appliqué work has been an important aspect of religious ceremony and secular festivals. It has decorated the garments and finery of aristocratic life; in its application to the adornment of national folk costumes and useful objects, it was an activity of great personal satisfaction and enjoyment.

Today, the techniques of the past are merging with the creative attitudes of the present, and at the same time, being modified by them. Contemporary work shows that all of the ancient techniques

**Figure 2.9**    Section of a patchwork quilt, about 1890, with numerous embroidery stitches accenting the sections of plain and printed cloth.

are valid when adapted to present-day design imagery and experimental forms. With a vigorous and unsentimental approach to the medium, uniquely expressive kinds of work have been completed, to be shared and enjoyed by all. Like all art activities, these also stem from the fundamental impulse to give form to and preserve ideas and feelings that have a personal meaning.

# 3 Tools and Materials

In our technological age, the materials and tools of art are so often thought to be of a very highly specialized nature, somehow removed from the kinds of objects we encounter and respond to in day-to-day living. In threads, yarns, and cloth, the medium of fibers, the concern is with materials that are familiar to everyone in many kinds of contexts. The tools, also, may already be a part of the general household supplies, or if not, are easily accessible.

Stitching and appliqué work does not require a large, fully equipped studio, but an adequate work space is necessary. A large worktable with good lighting is certainly important. There are many different ways of working in this medium and often the nature of the technique will suggest its own appropriate studio arrangement.

Some craftsmen prefer to work comfortably seated, others prefer the floor, and some work best standing up, with the piece in progress suspended from the ceiling or flat on a table. Often, the cloth is mounted on some type of frame or stretcher, but it can be worked loosely in the hand, also. There is no one way that is better than any

**Figure 3.1**    Skeins, balls, and spools of yarn in a random
assortment provides inspiration for combining colors, weights,
and textures.

other because the manner of working is often just as personal as the
work itself.

One of the most appealing aspects of working in the various
stitching and appliqué techniques is in the discovery and use of the
enormous range of available materials. In both yarns and cloth,
choices can be made from an amazing selection, offering great
diversity in color, texture, pattern, and weight.

## YARNS

Definitions of yarns should not be limiting factors. Any material that
can be used to form stitches, that can be threaded through the eye of
a needle or attached to a background cloth, is potentially useful
when you are designing wall hangings and related expressive objects.

In exploring the vast selection of yarns, cords, and threads that
can be used in stitching, first become familiar with the many varieties
available in department stores and shops that stock knitters' supplies.
Here, large skeins of knitting worsted can be found in both wool and
synthetic fibers, often in as many as fifty colors. This is a soft, supple

**Figure 3.2**   An assortment of yarns of many weights and textures.

**Figure 3.3**   Sample cards of weaving yarns showing color selection available.

yarn, usually four-ply and ideally suited to stitching on backgrounds of medium- to heavyweight fabric, not too tightly woven. The four-ply weight can be split into two-ply strands for a thinner yarn. The vast color range provides the palest tints to the most vibrant hues; in neutrals, too, there are several tones of white, soft beiges, and grays.

Readily available are plain yarns used for crocheting and finer threads used for machine sewing. Embroidery floss, a many-stranded cotton packaged in small skeins, can be found in most department stores and, again, in numerous colors. These are materials that can be obtained locally with little difficulty and present an excellent assortment for both the beginner and the more experienced worker.

When yarns, cords, and threads of more unusual character are wanted, they can be ordered from sources that supply hand weavers. Several of these companies are listed on page 147-48, with additional addresses found by browsing through advertisements in *Craft Horizons* and *Shuttle, Spindle and Dyepot* magazines. There is usually a small charge for the set of sample cards, but these provide an invaluable introduction to the enormous variety of yarns available and become an important reference in planning future work.

In most cases these yarns will be very different from those obtained locally. The range of novelty yarns is especially interesting with its highly textured, knotted, loop, and ratiné types. Bulky yarns, often having a rough, handspun quality, are inspiring in themselves, as are beautiful slub yarns, their uneven spinning resulting in a thick and thin surface effect. In addition, hanks of unspun fleece can be obtained, as well as raffia, metallic, and plastic yarns.

Although each type of thread, yarn, or cord available was prepared for a particular purpose, all are potentially valuable for stitching. With familiarity comes a more acute awareness of the unique surface qualities of each type, and with actual practice in making stitches, this awareness is continually refined. Because yarns differ so greatly in weight, in texture, and in color, they are always visually stimulating and a joy to collect and to use.

## CLOTH

The tremendous variety available in cloth made today is, like yarn, almost endless in its diversity. There are so many fibers, both natural and manufactured, so many weave structures, weights, patterns, colors, and textural surfaces, that the assortment seems overwhelming. In selecting cloth for work in stitching and appliqué, the design and character of the work itself will often suggest the types of fabric most appropriate.

**Figure 3.4**  Contrasts in fiber, pattern, and weave are evident in
this assortment of small pieces of fabric.

Hunting for fabrics can be an adventure in itself, especially when
you are attempting to search out exotic materials from second-hand
stores and rummage counters. Compared with this, shopping in retail
stores may not seem as glamorous but it is often necessary if several
uniformly consistent yards of a particular kind of cloth are required.
While fabric can be purchased because the "look" or the "feel" of
the cloth seems appropriate, some knowledge about the specific
kinds of materials available will be helpful. This information is useful
in identifying fabrics collected at random.

Selecting cloth as a background for stitching calls for different
considerations than when using the fabric for surface appliqué, or for
assembled or constructed pieces. When stitching methods are to be
used, backgrounds are most effective when the textural surface is
subdued, serving as a background rather than a competitive element
to the yarns. Plain weave or weaves that are evenly structured allow
the varied surface qualities of the stitching to project. Fabrics that
are visually interesting in themselves are usually not appropriate for
all-over backgrounds but can be used in sections as appliqué.

If bulky yarns are to be used in the stitching, the weave of the
cloth should not be too tightly constructed; large needles should be
pulled through the cloth without undue strain. This is also true of
the punch needle if areas of hooking are to be incorporated into the

work. If specific yarns have been chosen, you should bring these along when you are shopping and place them on various fabrics considered for backgrounds, so that you can observe color and textural contrasts.

Specific types of cloth can be recognized by weave surface and yarn structure, but it is not uncommon to find similar fabrics in both natural and manufactured fibers. For example, both cotton and rayon velveteen are available; organdy is made in cotton, nylon, and dacron. Some manufactured fibers are very close in appearance to wool and linen; these are used a great deal in upholstery fabrics. These rayons, nylons, acrylics, dacrons, to cite only a few, not only resemble natural fibers but in many instances are equally satisfactory. Some fabrics are obviously synthetic. Stretch knits, transparent nylons, fiber glass, and plastic cloth add additional diversity.

Some very basic types of fabrics that could be considered appropriate as background material for stitching and appliqué work are:

### WOOL

Woven woolen cloth offers the greatest range of possibilities in color, weave structure, and weight. It is an ideal background for stitching and some types of appliqué, especially if the design requires a firm yet luxurious cloth with rich coloration. Selection can be made from a variety of weights, depending on the types of yarns being used in the stitching and the nature of the design. Dress weights are light, some semitransparent; flannels are quite densely woven, suitable for fine detailing; and coating weights are strong and heavy, appropriate for hooking and bold stitching.

### FELT

Felt is a sturdy cloth, usually made of wool fibers but not woven in the traditional method of warp/weft interlacing. Instead, the fibers are permanently matted and fused together in a special process called "felting." The surface is soft, flat, and smooth. Felt is a favorite material for banners and large hangings, ideal for use as backgrounds and applied sections. Since it is not woven, cut edges never ravel. The cloth is so dense, however, that hand sewing is difficult unless very

**Figure 3.5** Burlap, wool, linen, viscose rayon (top to bottom).

fine, strong needles are used. Machine stitching is more efficient. Many beautiful colors are available which can be ordered directly from commercial suppliers if not found locally.

## LINEN

Linen has a long history of use in traditional embroidery techniques and is certainly suitable for contemporary work in stitching and appliqué. It is a firm, very durable fabric, woven in several different weights. Linen has a rather limited color range, compared to wool and cotton, but it is really most effective in its neutral tones. Sometimes this cloth can be found locally in drapery departments, but the best selections can be made from suppliers of unsized artist's canvas. It should be noted that cloth called "butcher linen" is actually of a rayon fiber woven to resemble linen.

## BURLAP

Jute, a coarse natural fiber, is used in the making of burlap. This is a stiff, loosely woven fabric available in natural and a wide selection of colors. In appearance, burlap would seem to be an ideal background cloth for stitching and appliqué, but it is really not durable. After several years, the fiber may begin to rot, although a few coats of clear acrylic spray will be helpful in this regard. Also, the colors will tend to fade quickly if exposed continually to direct sunlight. While burlap is fine for initial experiments, more durable and colorfast materials are suggested for serious work.

## COTTON

The cotton textiles available today offer a wealth of choices in plain weave cloth both in solid colors and multicolored prints. Medium-weight cottons, called percale or broadcloth, are frequently used in flat appliqué and are especially effective in cutwork methods. These fabrics are often woven with a percentage of synthetic yarn for crease resistance. Unbleached muslins have been used as backgrounds, and osnaburg, a somewhat coarser cloth made in several weights, is excellent for both stitching and appliqué. Osnaburg is used for sacking cement and can be purchased from bag manufacturers. Some lighter-weight cottons are organdy, lawn, and batiste; heavier types are sailcloth, hopsacking, duck, and monk's cloth.

**Figure 3.6** *Encounter* (12" x 15"), by Cheryl Eng. This panel combines many different types of cloth. The background is wool felt, the wings sheer dacron formed over wire, with other sections in cotton and printed rayon.

These are very basic types of cloth. There are, in addition, numerous fabrics of a more specialized nature. Sheer cloth is structurally thin, with a very fine, delicate quality. Fabrics with a smooth surface are usually woven in plain weave, while others have a more meshlike appearance. Some are transparent, while others are starched for additional body. A few of the more familiar types of sheer fabrics are: batiste, chiffon, crinoline, gauze, marquisette, voile, netting, and organdy.

The surface of satin is unusually smooth and shiny, reflecting the light. Taffeta is also very smooth, as are many lightweight nylons and other synthetics. There are fabrics with a soft, luxurious surface appearance because of the pile effect in the weaving. These are velvets, velours, and corduroys. Brocades are quite heavy, woven with prominent, complex design motifs.

The fabrics described here represent more of a general summary than a complete listing and are intended primarily as a guide for purchase and use.

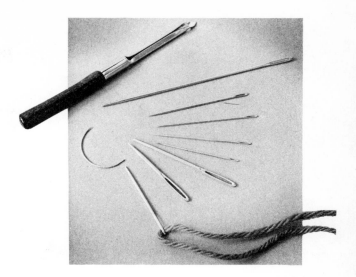

# 4 Needles and Notions

Several types of needles are available which are useful for different kinds of stitching and appliqué work. In selecting needles, it is really not important to be familiar with all of the terminology and size ranges. Very often, simply observing the needle itself will determine whether or not it will be appropriate for the work.

For the beginner, some very general guides might be helpful. Whatever the size, needles should be strong and have a large enough eye so that the yarn or thread fits through easily, without forcing or splitting. Logically, coarse, heavy fabrics call for larger, heavier needles; for lighter weights of cloth, thin but fairly long needles are best. With the proper needle, the stitches can be worked efficiently, without strain or awkwardness, and the experience is much more enjoyable.

Large crewel or embroidery needles will probably be most useful; these are made in several different sizes. Tapestry needles are shorter and heavier. They have a long eye, but are blunt rather than sharp and are designed for use on canvas or cloth with an open-weave structure. Chenille needles are somewhat similar, except that they

**Figure 4.1**    Different types of needles used for stiching and a
punch rug needle for hooking.

have sharper points. Very long needles are called mattress needles
and are excellent for interweaving with the background cloth. As one
works, an ample selection of many needles of different sizes should
be readily at hand.

For hooking, a punch needle or hand hook is necessary. Other
useful items are scissors, pins, hoops, and frames.

In both stitching and appliqué work, it may be necessary to
stretch the cloth onto a hoop or frame to provide sufficient work
area for the stitching. Small hoops can be used but they are not
practical for larger sections of cloth, since they must be moved about
so frequently that it is difficult to gain a sense of the design as a
whole. Larger hoops, sometimes called tambours, are more suitable.

Rectangular frames can be used also, and these can be quite simply
constructed of soft wood; many craftsmen prefer the canvas
stretcher frames with mitered corners cut so that they can be easily
fitted together. The cloth should be tacked to the sides of the frame
following a straight thread alignment. For a good working surface,
there is no need to pull the cloth too tightly. In fact, an overly taut
surface will not allow the necessary "give" required for efficient
stitching, and the handling of the needle becomes very awkward.

If the panel is to be permanently mounted on a frame when
finished, it should be untacked and then restretched with a much
more taut surface.

There are also frames on stands, really designed for rug making,
but very practical for the temporary stretching of large pieces of
cloth.

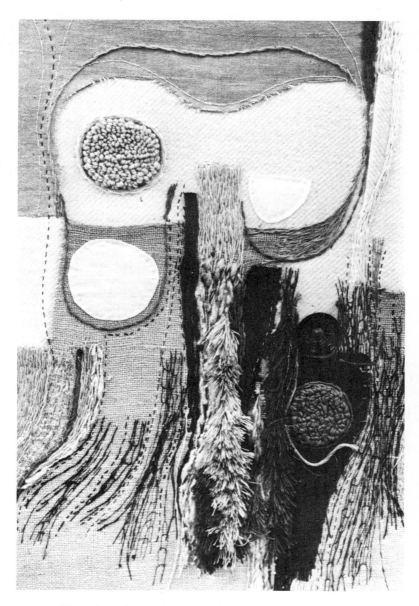

**Figure 4.2** Detail of textile panel by the author showing several basic stitches, with appliqué of burlap and linen on a white wool background. The punch needle was used for the areas of hooking.

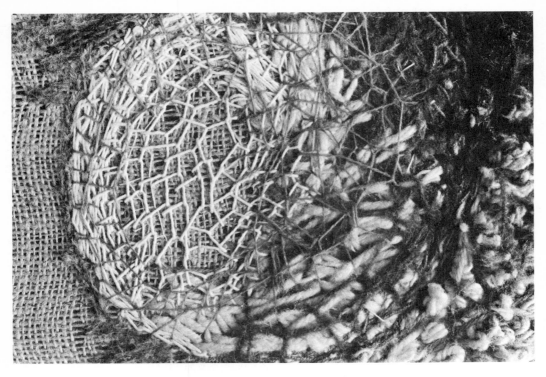

**Figure 4.3**    Detail with controlled rows of straight stitching; although the shapes vary, the alignment is precise.

**Figure 4.4**    Detail with free overlapping of the blanket stitch; yarns of both wool and cotton are used.

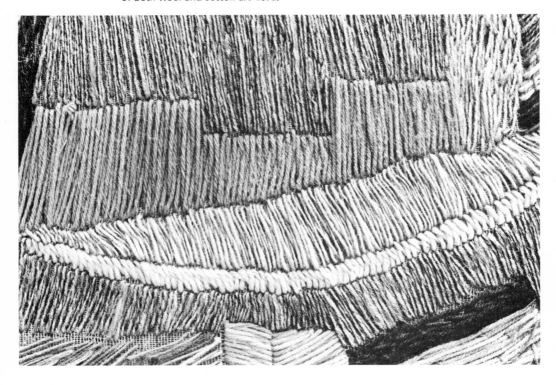

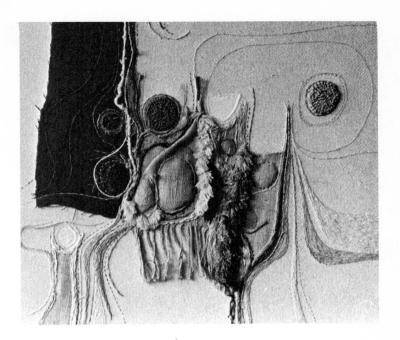

# 5 Stitches and Stitching

Yarns and sections of cloth can be attached to the background fabric in many different ways, resulting in many different kinds of effects. This is essentially what stitching is all about—using the yarns functionally and in ways that emphasize the unique visual and tactile qualities of the material.

Stitching can also provide a means of building shape and form relationships within the work. When the same stitch is repeated to cover a substantial area, its unit structure becomes hidden; the stitch is not seen by itself but is a small part of an overall surface effect. When worked in this manner, the most simple stitch takes on a new interest because of the way it is used.

This is as true of historic and traditional work as it is of contemporary. The embroidered cloths from ancient Peru show the stem stitch used, as well as a form of darning over the base fabric. The stitches were worked close together. Often, for filling shapes, rows of stitches were worked into the previous row without being caught into the background cloth. Buttonhole stitches were also used, as were fringes and tassels made by needle methods.

25

**Figure 5.1**     A stitched and hooked panel, by Michelle Potter, using
a variety of simple stitches on a burlap background.

In the rhythmic floral patterns of traditional crewel embroidery,
the chain stitch was used extensively, along with the stem and
buttonhole stitch. Groupings of French knots added surface variation
and the satin stitch, an alignment of straight line stitches, was used to
fill in small shapes. When a stitch is repeated many times within a
fairly small area, its individuality gives way to the stronger effect of
the cluster or grouping.

This is seldom the case in appliqué methods, in which the visual
character of the stitch itself becomes an important surface embellishment. Here, the necessary contrast is achieved by isolating the
individual stitch; the structure of the stitch becomes part of the
design. Considered in this way, even the simple in-and-out trailing of
the running stitch takes on clarity and prominence. Stitching can add
detail and richness to cloth without becoming a dominating textural
shape.

In addition to some of the basic stitches described here, it is
possible to find dictionaries or charts illustrating many more variations. These are intriguing but can be overwhelming, too, especially if
one thinks it necessary to learn or memorize all of these before any

"real" work can begin. This is not the case. Certainly, it is logical to understand several basic stitches; simple skills are required for this. However, it is not so much the mastery of knowing how to make the stitch that is important, but the more intuitive understanding of how to apply and utilize the particular stitch most effectively in the design of the work.

In carefully reviewing the various completed examples illustrated, it becomes evident that in many of the pieces, surprisingly few different stitches are actually used. After one becomes familiar with many kinds of stitches, initially, it often happens that only a certain few are retained and used consistently and effectively. To the artists, these few stitches become a kind of personal vocabulary, used again and again in their numerous subtleties and variations.

While an extensive knowledge of many different kinds of stitches is certainly not required for excellent work, it is important to understand the kinds of stitches that are most appropriate for the particular kinds of surface effects wanted in the design. Stitching is the means for achieving these effects. This indicates a need for exploring and experimenting with needles and yarns, always keeping in mind that effects of remarkable richness can be achieved with very few stitches used effectively.

**Figure 5.2**   Detail of a stitchery panel in progress. Numerous stitches overlapped to achieve surface richness.

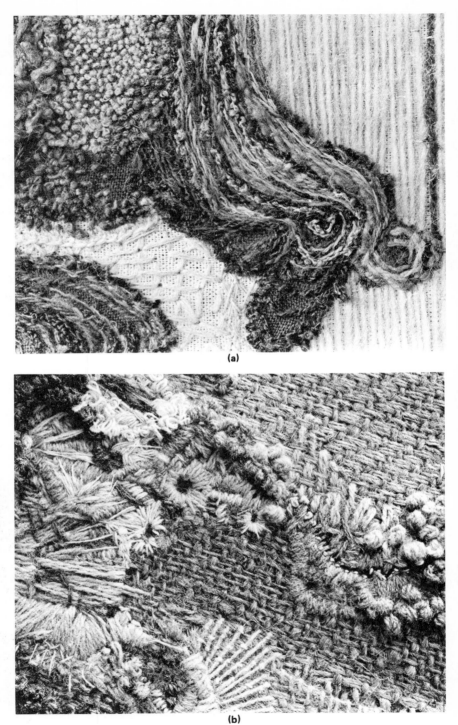

(a)

(b)

**Figure 5.3** Details showing a close-up view of several kinds of
stitches, including French knots.

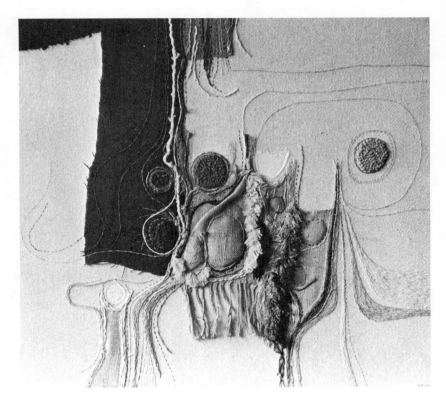

**Figure 5.4** *Wall and Vine* (36″ x 36″), by the author is a combination of many techniques. Appliqué, stitching, hooking, and padding have all been utilized.

**Figure 5.5** Detail showing the couching of heavy Mexican yarn to the background of woolen cloth.

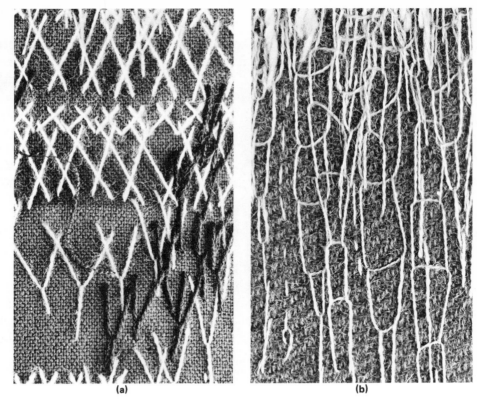

(a)

(b)

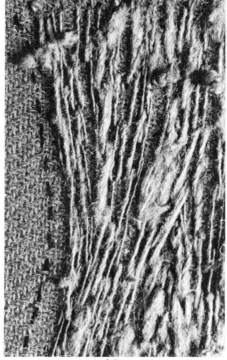

**Figure 5.6** Small samples
illustrating some basic stitches.

(c)

For the beginner, introductory experiences need not begin with kits or completely prescribed sets of directions; these place undue importance on technical perfection, rather than encouraging creative attitudes toward designing and developing ideas. Far more valuable are simple exercises or samples that allow the individual to become familiar with some of the different kinds of stitches, and realize their possibilities in ways that are conducive to the development of his or her own personal sense of growth. Working in this way, one will be able to observe first-hand how the character of every stitch will change with differing weights of yarn and different background fabric. Size and scale will change as relationships begin to emerge, and differing densities will occur as the stitch is repeated. It will be possible to work for a very long time without exhausting the possibilities of one single stitch.

To begin, gather together a random assortment of yarns and threads, some needles of different sizes, and for background, a section of cloth about two feet square. The cloth should not be too tightly woven, so that large needles can be used with ease. If the cloth is tacked to a frame or stretched in a large hoop, it will be easier to work with the needle because the taut background supports the stitches.

At this stage it is not necessary to plan or prepare sketches. Simply begin, starting with a basic linear stitch, such as the stem stitch, and work in a series of rows over the surface of the cloth. The needle really functions as a drawing tool. Place some of the rows of stitched lines close together, others further apart, trying to sense the relationship of the space to the stitches as the work progresses.

While working, change the yarn, trying both fine and bulky varieties, adjusting the length of the stitch to what seems most appropriate for the weight of the yarn. Introduce other essentially linear stitches into the sample, such as the running stitch and the back stitch; try couching some heavier yarns onto the background cloth.

Although this is a learning exercise, seemingly with no plan or design, observe the stitches carefully as they begin to build shapes and patterns on the cloth. The rows can be aligned in an up and down manner, side to side, or intersecting at different angles. If the sample seems to take on its own design, try to guide the direction, sensing the difference between complexity and confusion.

On another experimental sample, work with several different stitches, this time in close groupings so that variations in surface quality can be observed. Open and closed chain stitches, buttonhole and vandyke stitches can be explored in this manner. One of the

Running Stitch

Stem or Outline Stitch

Straight Stitch

Satin Stitch

Chain Stitch

Open Chain or Ladder Stitch

Blanket Stitch

Couching

French Knot

Back Stitch

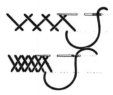

Herringbone Stitch

Cross Stitch

**Figure 5.7**    Running Stitch, Stem or Outline Stitch, Straight Stitch,
Satin Stitch, Chain Stitch, Open Chain or Ladder Stitch, Blanket
Stitch, Couching, French Knot, Back Stitch, Herringbone Stitch,
Cross Stitch

**Figure 5.8**  Detail of random stitching using many different kinds of yarn.

**Figure 5.9**  *Royal Couple*  (30" x 30"), by Philip Smith. Simple straight stitching was effectively used in this colorful panel.

discoveries resulting from working the stitches in clusters is that the distinctiveness of each type of yarn becomes evident, contributing greatly to the overall textural effect.

Knowledge of yarns develops hand in hand with this initial practice in working with stitches. Using different types of yarn, work the same stitch in a close, flat manner, or in a very open, lacelike effect. Plied or many-stranded yarns can be separated; thinner yarns and threads can be used with several strands grouped together.

Ideas for additional samples, combining more varied stitches, will come about naturally. The more complex stitches are variations of a few basic types. It should be remembered, too, that each stitch can be developed beyond its normally accepted appearance, so that its character is changed. Considered in this way, each stitch can become a starting point for inventing new variations, perhaps leading to entirely new stitches.

When some of the basic stitches are familiar, try working several in ways that are somewhat different from the usual, accepted manner. Exaggerate the stitch by lengthening the strokes far beyond what would be normal, or deliberately shorten or widen the entire stitch. Stitches that are frequently worked in a more or less similar size can be worked in an irregular manner with the sizes constantly changing. In some cases, it is possible to detach stitches that are usually interrelated.

From these small, improvised samples, a familiarity and confidence in using stitches gradually develops. The results are a helpful reference for future work and are often beautiful in themselves.

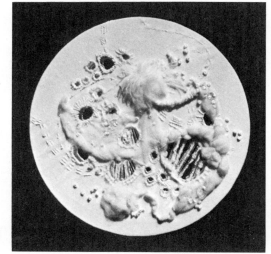

**Figure 5.10** In *White Series* (14″ d.), I. C. Jackson Brockette works relieflike stitch effects around cut openings in a background of bonded white wool. A circular mirror is mounted behind the fabric.

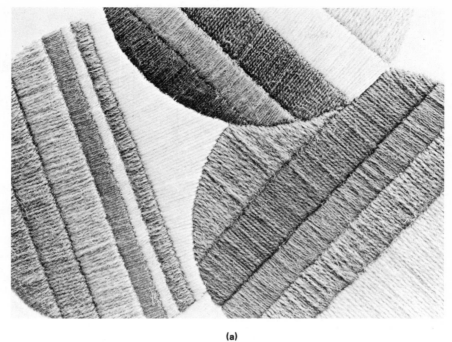

(a)

(b)

**Figure 5.11**    Two contrasting approaches to stitching: above,
planned and highly controlled; below; freely spontaneous.

**Figure 5.12** *Genesis I* (40" x 28"), by Eileen Collins. Meticulous craftsmanship and subtle color mark this appliqué panel. Both plain and printed fabrics are used, embellished with surface stitching and padding.

# 6 Appliqué Methods

By definition, appliqué means to "apply," to attach one material to another. An orientation with the vocabulary of the painter would probably suggest the term, "collage," and in current exhibitions of textiles the terms "cloth-collage" and "appliqué" seem to be used interchangeably to describe work that incorporates applied areas of cloth or fiber to a background material. Fabric-collage implies a relation to assemblage or multilayered constructions of cloth with other appropriate materials. It is a term consistent with new attitudes about using and combining materials and suggests a fusion of many methods and techniques.

When a clarity of definition is wanted, collage originally referred to the use of an adhesive or glue type of bonding to join one material to another, while traditionally, appliqué implies the use of stitching to join one cloth section to another. The contemporary textile artist is less concerned with maintaining precise definitions than with using the cloth as an expressive material, abandoning long-established "methods" for a freedom to explore new ideas and invent new forms with cloth.

**Figure 6.1** In preparing a design for a large appliqué banner, shapes of cut paper are placed on the background fabric and moved about until the best arrangement is achieved.

**Figure 6.2** The paper shapes are used as patterns in cutting the cloth.

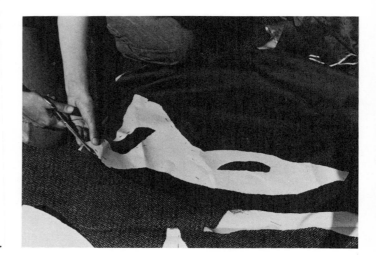

**Figure 6.3** Chalk lines mark the hems on the appliqué sections. These will be turned back prior to final pinning and stitching.

**Figure 6.4** A love of horses inspired this mural size appliqué wall hanging (5' x 8') (shown in detail) by Susan Wilke. On a background of white cotton sailcloth, both plain and printed fabrics are used; the linear work is drawn in with a felt-tip marker.

There are several variations of appliqué, with each method having its own unique qualities. Although all appliqué techniques are a heritage from the past, the diverse ways in which they are used in contemporary work show how adaptable they are to changing ideas and modes of working. Traditional terms, such as onlaid and inlaid appliqué, have a rather old-fashioned connotation since they are used primarily in reference to historical museum pieces of decorative rather than expressive interest. However, since so many present-day textile artists utilize these methods in one form or another, a brief review might be helpful in recognizing the basic types.

In the onlaid methods the design motif of one material is cut out and then placed on a background fabric, with some type of needlework applied to form a secure attachment. This simple description, however, does not convey the amazing versatility in finding ways to finish off the edges so the cloth does not fray.

**Figure 6.5** *Pied Piper* (30″ x 24″),
by Malcolm McCormack. Appliqué of felt,
velvet, and burlap was used for this panel.
The stitching is in raffia and wool.

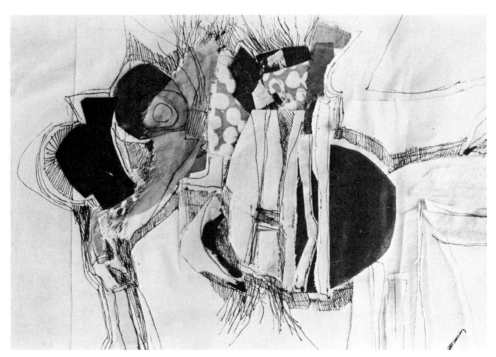

**Figure 6.6** Drawing with pen and black ink provides a dominant
linear quality that relates the cloth appliqué shapes in this panel by
Joanne Ross. The background is off-white cotton.

In numerous examples of historic European costume decoration, metallic yarns were carefully couched around the cloth shapes, securing them to the background. On large heraldic banners and ecclesiastical hangings of the Middle Ages, braided cords or decorative, narrow bands of ribbon were used to hold the applied cloth in place. Strings of fine beading were also used for this purpose, contributing additional interest and textural richness.

In appliqué work where shapes of cloth are attached to a background, the treatment of fabric edges is an important factor in establishing the surface character of the design and in the more technical aspects of the workmanship. In addition to couching or superimposing a cord or braid around the edges of the motif, embroidery stitches can also be used. One row, or several rows, of closely placed buttonhole or chain stitching can be worked around the edges of the applied portions of cloth. The stitches hold the fabric in place but also add a great deal to the richness of the overall surface. This approximates the effects obtained when close zigzag machine stitching is used in contemporary work on large banners and wall hangings.

In early American quilts, appliqué techniques were used, with the carefully cut shapes of cloth attached to the background fabric by

**Figure 6.7**    Detail from an American quilt, about 1890. Each portion of the star shape was carefully cut from printed cotton and attached to the base with blind stitching.

the use of small but very firm stitches. Here, the raw cut edges of each piece of cloth to be applied are carefully turned back to avoid fraying, with blind stitching used for a secure fastening of one section of cloth to the other. With this method, the pattern or surface quality of the cloth is emphasized rather than the stitching.

The running stitch is also very appropriate for attaching appliqué sections when the edges of the shapes are turned back. Since a portion of this stitch does appear on the top surface of the cloth, it does affect the overall character of the design, although in a very subtle way. When used functionally, simply to attach, the stitch closely parallels the outline of the shape. However, it should be kept in mind that this stitch, like all embroidery stitches, can be used within the applied sections of the design, adding new decorative elements.

A related quilting technique is patchwork. This method of working with cloth implies the piecing together of many small pieces of fabric to form a newly structured material. The pioneer quilt makers,

**Figure 6.8** Patchwork "crazy" quilt, about 1890. Scraps of oddly shaped cloth were sewn together for the top of the quilt, with fancy embroidery stitches adding further interest.

**Figure 6.9**  A whale hunt is the subject of this mola from San Blas, Panama, in the familiar layered cutwork technique.

motivated more by thrift than beauty, used odd scraps of cloth, strange shapes left over from a previous sewing project and still durable pieces cut from worn articles of clothing. The term "crazy quilt" was used to identify this type of work. The best of these quilts are valued today for their wonderful vitality; they are conglomerates of infinite surface variation and, therefore, are never dull.

Another traditional appliqué method given new interpretation by today's textile artists calls for the cutting away of design motif shapes from a ground material. This exposes another color or another type of cloth from underneath. Historically, this technique was often used in very elaborate designs on wall hangings, altar panels, and the richly embellished garments worn at court by the aristocracy. Velvets, satins, and other exotic fabrics were used, with the edges finished off with gold cord or braid couched around the outline of each shape.

Primitive peoples in different parts of the world have evolved variations of this method. The women of the San Blas Islands near

Panama have long been known for their textile appliqué work. These are the intricate layered appliqué blouse pieces called molas. By stacking several layers of cotton cloth, each the same size but a different color, the design can be cut out from the top layer or through several layers, revealing different colors in different sections of the piece. Occasionally, small shapes are applied directly to the surface, with all raw cut edges turned under and carefully blind stitched.

The traditional subject-matter motifs are stylized bird, animal, human, and plant forms, sometimes incorporated with a background of slitlike shapes. In recent years, the many tourists who visit the islands have been collecting these molas; some are considered museum pieces. Certain elements of current American culture have been introduced to the islands, influencing the designs on the textiles. Now, along with the familiar imagery, there are molas with interpretations of Mickey Mouse, Santa Claus, and Batman.

In addition to these basic methods, there are other variations of appliqué which reflect attitudes very much in keeping with the current movements in contemporary art. These influences have inspired textile artists to exploit some of the natural qualities of cloth often overlooked in more traditional ways of working. Cloth is a flat material, but it is also pliable and can easily be manipulated in the hand into well-defined forms. These can be attached to backgrounds by stitching, with stuffing used in some areas for more pronounced raised surfaces.

Cloth folds readily; it can be crushed, gathered, twisted, coiled, and pleated. All of these characteristics of fabric can be used to advantage in building relief effects in cloth constructions and assemblages. Edges of cut cloth can be left free to ravel; the loose threads are often appropriate to the design. In many of these pieces, rich surface stitching works with the applied areas of cloth, adding textural variation and becoming a significant part of the total image.

As the concept of appliqué continually grows, more and more experimental ideas take form in contemporary textile work. Exploring the values of transparent cloth effects opens up still more possibilities for variation in surface interest. Sheer gauze fabrics, organdy, chiffon, and open laces can be applied as overlays on opaque fabric, resulting in a change in color and in textural interest. Netting and veiling cloth are also excellent for partially shading out a color that is too blatant or for breaking up a solid area into smaller, more subtle facets.

On cloth that is not too tightly woven, portions of the warp or filler threads can be carefully cut and removed entirely, resulting in enclosed shapes or loosely hanging fringes.

Discovering and using these ideas is very much a part of designing and influences the developing image of the work. The manner in which the materials are used can set a definite direction or focus a mood. While the tiny, painstaking stitches of older work are often abandoned for a bolder exploitation of cloth itself, essential craftsmanship and concern for the material is of equal importance. Directness and honesty in building the design do not lessen the need for sensitivity and care in the workmanship.

**Figure 6.10**    This large appliqué panel, by Wendy Toogood, uses design motifs inspired by forms in children's paintings.

**Figure 6.11**    Remade Block Blanket
(9' x 7'), by Bonnie Gisel, is constructed
of numerous square units stitched
together in a patchwork fashion. It is
monochromatic in color, in tones of
green dyed by the artist.

**Figure 6.12**    This detail shows how a
square shape was cut out of each of the
original units and a contrasting cloth
attached from behind each opening.
Striped and printed fabrics as well as
hand-gathered cloth were used.

**Figure 6.13** *Country Cupboard*
(30" x 24"), by Randi Stevelman.
Printed cloth as appliqué is seen in
this panel.

**Figure 6.14** A sample showing the
juxtaposition of printed fabric; the small
floral print is seen next to stripes of
varying widths.

**Figure 6.15** *Winter Elegy* (54″ x 20″), by the author contains sections of appliqué as well as drawn thread fringe, padding, and stitching.

**Figure 6.16** *Angel's Folly* (21″ x 20″), by Joan Blumenbaum. Appliqué in felt, velour, and striped cotton were used in designing this panel. Silk-screen printing and machine embroidery are seen in the circular shape in the center.

**Figure 6.17** Detail of *Angel's Folly.*

# 7 Notes on Designing

Designing in stitching and appliqué techniques is, like any creative endeavor, not easily described in terms of step-by-step directions. The approach suggested here is flexible enough to provide a kind of framework for individual growth and development. There is no quick, foolproof path to easy success, because in designing, each individual is encouraged to find his or her own way. We learn best what we discover for ourselves.

In working with yarns and cloth, the richly varied qualities of the materials themselves will often provide the initial impetus, setting the first, tentative directions that the work will follow. However, this can occur only if we are truly receptive to these materials, so that we are able to make discerning choices among them and combine them in imaginative ways. This implies a sensitivity to all manner of fibers, yarns, threads, and cloth, and to their coloration, surface texture, and weight. It also implies a feeling for "putting things together," an awareness of contrast, rhythm, and proportion that is personal and reflects one's own attitudes and ideas.

Temperament and personality are important, too, in setting a predisposition toward one particular way of working, one particular range of materials. The expressive possibilities in stitching and appliqué are so great that it seems natural to want to become involved in those aspects toward which we seem instinctively attuned. Some will respond to the softness and delicacy of certain yarns, others to the coarse immediacy of ropes and twines. The transparency of some kinds of cloth can be inspiring, as can the shininess of satin, the rich depth of velvet.

This is apparent in choice of technique. Some will want to work exclusively with stitching, while others will combine stitching with cloth appliqué or collage, perhaps incorporating hooking or knotting techniques. An interest in cloth itself can open many avenues for personal involvement in the various kinds of appliqué techniques. Diversity in pattern and texture can be explored by the juxtaposition of pieces of printed cloth. Those with an interest in scluptural forms may turn to relief effects achieved by stuffing or by three-dimensional figures in cloth.

While it seems natural to prefer one technique or way of working over another, it should not be thought that the acquisition or mastery of technical skills will automatically result in excellent work.

**Figure 7.1**   A suggested landscape in simplified, abstract shapes, designed with velvet appliqué and surface stitching by Sylvia Fahey.

**Figure 7.2**    Straight satin stitches are combined with chain and blanket stitches. The raised loop shapes were worked with the punch needle.

Certainly, skills are important, for without them we do not have the necessary "know-how" to effectively translate our ideas into the medium. Technical ability cannot be valued for itself, but as the "means" of visualizing and giving form to our ideas. Without creative purpose, technical skill alone can lead to imitating the work of others or following through on other people's directions.

With some experience in designing and some confidence in handling the materials, the methods or means of working become as personal, as individualized as the ideas themselves; both technique and concept are entirely interdependent, one with the other. In designing for stitching and appliqué, it will be found that there is more to learn than stitches, more to understand than theoretical design principles. The approach described here aims toward a fusion of both technique and inventiveness, so that thinking creatively within the medium becomes an inseparable adjunct to the growth of technical skills.

Designing has often been defined as a process of making choices and, as such, has analogies to the kind of decision-making activities we experience daily. In living, one constantly makes choices, applying functional, ethical, or perhaps artistic considerations. These choices are not made mindlessly, but are appropriate to personal

51

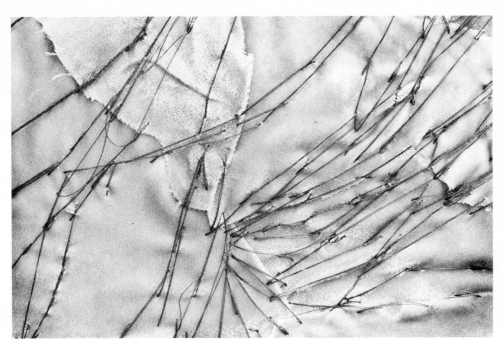

**Figure 7.3**    Detail opposite panel. A close-up view of stem stitches over the velvet; the fine thread is used doubled.

standards, attitudes, and beliefs. In designing, also, the conscious selection of one color over another, of one tactile surface over another, or of one technical variation over another is an exercise of judgment and preference.

When experience and training are limited, when confidence is lacking, these choices supposedly based on esthetic considerations are not truly personal; instead they become overly influenced by current promotional vogues or passing styles. Ideas, however, require individual interpretation if the work is to have value as art. No real design solutions are necessary in order to duplicate the work of someone else.

It is possible to be so conditioned by trite and banal examples that we approach our materials with preconceived notions about how certain stitches are to be used, or about what themes or subject matter is suitable. Pretty flowers again? An open attitude to new ideas and fresh approaches is of great importance.

In this medium, like any other, learning comes about by doing. Starting with a varied assortment of yarns and cloth and a basic understanding of several stitches, initial experiments can be made. Without preliminary planning, try to build effective arrangements of line and shape formations, continually observing how the yarns and stitches interrelate with the background. Cut some simple shapes from scrap pieces of cloth and place them at random on the background. These shapes, of different colors and textures, will break up the space in very decisive ways. Move them about, studying their effect on the areas of stitching as well as the overall boundary of the background.

With these first beginnings, the initial grouping of stitches or pinning down of some cut shapes of cloth, the processes of designing begin. Even at this early stage, each beginning becomes a kind of nucleus of everything that is done subsequently. Sometimes it is possible to logically analyze the direction of the design, but often it is a trial and error procedure that we evaluate intuitively. From one group of stitches, another is suggested; one idea leads to another and

**Figure 7.4**    In *Girl Resting*    (24" x 24"), Ann DiMeo translates the seated figure into a stitched composition of unusual grace and refinement.

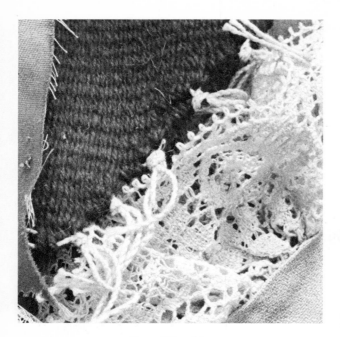

Figure 7.5　(a)

Figure 7.5　(b)

each choice in color, shape, tactile surface, or linear direction prepares the way for the next.

For a beginner, making a start often seems a formidable venture because in stitching and appliqué, the final results seem so complex in form and so richly varied in visual interest. It should be remembered that this kind of complexity can evolve from very humble beginnings. With some experience, the tonal and tactile diversity of the medium becomes evident. Working directly with the materials leads to first-hand discoveries about yarns and cloth, and into the kind of thinking that allows an individual to slowly find his or her own direction and potential.

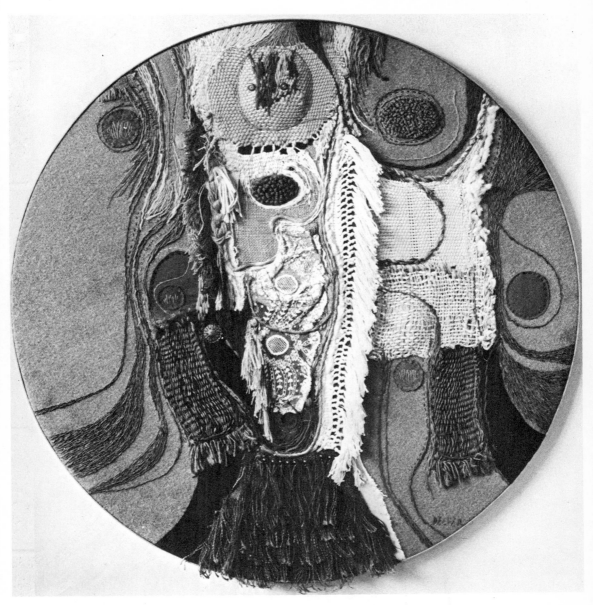

**Figure 7.6**   *Masked Figure*   (36" d.), by the author combines fragments of lace, fringe, beads, buttons, and hand-woven cloth to suggest a vaguely historical personage.

(a)

(b)

**Figure 7.7**    Sketches from the author's notebook. Studies in line, shape, and textural transitions suggest ideas for designs that can be expressed with yarns and cloth.

**Plate 1**
*Votive Form* (author)

**Plate 2**
*Pied Piper,* detail (Malcolm McCormack)

**Plate 3**
*Vest* (Suzanne Katz)

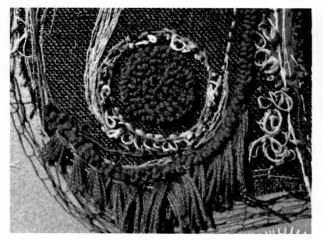

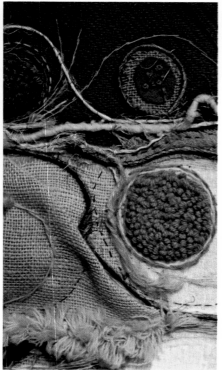

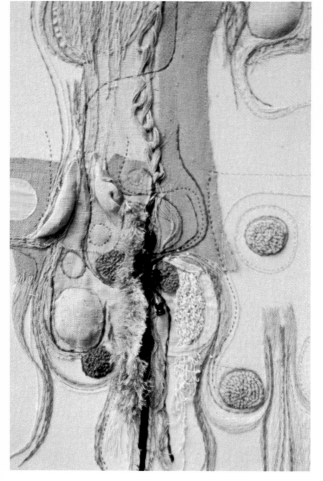

**Plate 4**
**Plate 5**
**Plate 6**
Details from work by the author

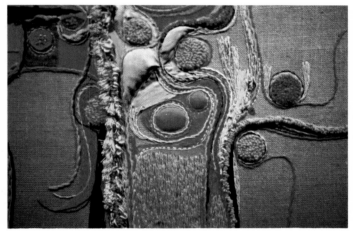

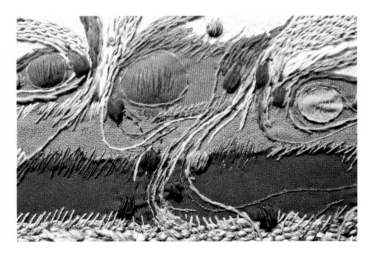

Plate 7
Plate 8
Plate 9

**Plate 10**  *Strata* (Sylvia Fahey)

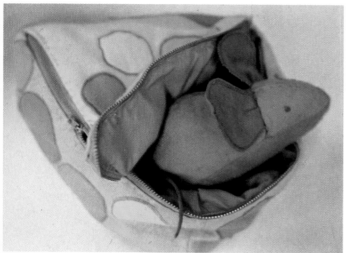

**Plate 11**  *Mouse and Cheese* (Carol Schwartzott)

**Plate 12**  *Insect Form* (Charlotte Cippola)

**Plate 13**
*Elusive Prey* (Susan Oyler)

**Plate 14**   *Stitched Form* (Helen Bitar)

**Plate 17** *Stitched Form—Bird* (Helen Bitar)

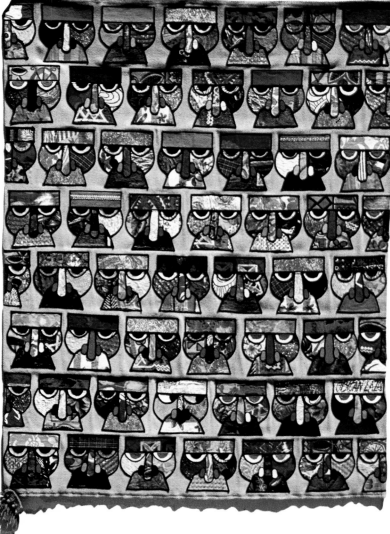

**Plate 18**
*Faces,* 58″ x 48″ (Lazar Obican)

**Plate 19**
Head with Hair (Lenore Davis)

**Plate 20**
*Pouch Form* (Carol Schwartzott)

**Plate 21**
*October Field* (author)

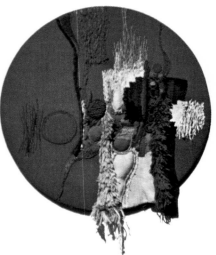

**Plate 22**
*Royal Family,* 36″ x 40″
(Jody Klein)

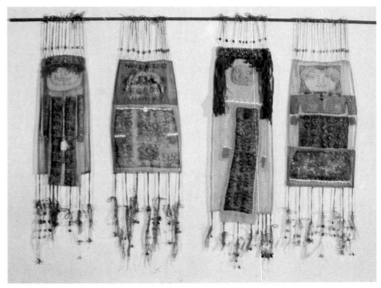

# 8 Ideas and Images

Materials themselves are a stimulating source of ideas. The introductory experiments previously suggested help make one aware of this. In stitching and appliqué, the kinds of materials we enjoy using most have a very strong motivational influence on the nature and the character of the images that evolve.

If the expressive quality of our work is to continually grow and the scope of our imagination to increase, it becomes necessary to bring to the work many kinds of ideas that can be interpreted in many different, yet personal ways. It seems almost too easy to say that the sources for these ideas are everywhere, all around us, all the time. Yes, ideas are everywhere, but the statement is meaningless unless we are aware of them and are prepared to "find" them. Sources for ideas can exist only if we are attuned to what we are looking for and ready to absorb what is essential.

People see things in different ways; what is important to one may be completely irrelevant to another. The artist, unlike the neutral observer, is always aware of the artistic potential in everything he encounters. If we intend to find ideas, we must know how to look

(a)

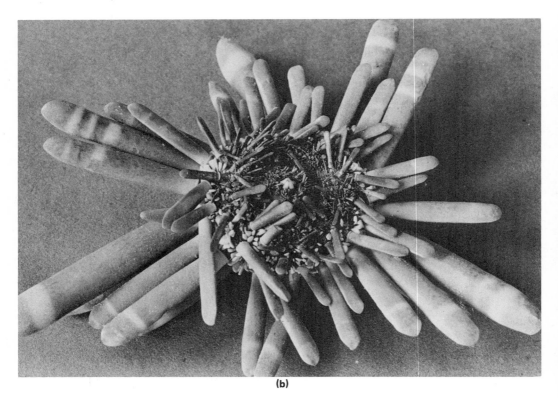

(b)

**Figure 8.1**    Natural forms provide an inexhaustible source of
imagery.

for them. Many experiments have indicated that we look casually at many things without really seeing anything.

Learning to look at what is around us deeply, thoroughly, and with a conscious intent to retain something of what is seen is a valuable habit that encourages the development of a creative attitude. For example, in walking over sidewalk, arriving at the destination could, for a short time, become secondary to examining the shapes of cracks in the concrete. An oil-slick puddle is not an unpleasant hurdle to be quickly jumped over, but a source of fantastic color and shape variations that could be mentally recorded, perhaps sketched out, and later remembered.

With careful observation, we can discover everywhere visual elements that transform vague thoughts into ideas and images to interpret and express through stitching and appliqué. All manner of relationships in colors, lines, shapes, and forms are around us all the time. The effort to seek out these qualities and give them new meaning is a rewarding task.

The examples of work illustrated show many kinds of imagery; imagination is not limited by concept or by material. It would be misleading to try to accurately pinpoint the exact sources of the idea for each of these pieces because artistic ideas are rarely dependent on one factor alone. Rather, the resulting work is a fusion of many related observations, attitudes, and experiences, tied together with a working sense of the materials and what the materials can do. The idea must be visualized, given form, and expressed through the materials.

Inspiration often begins with a searching out of those natural forms, objects, or arrangements that somehow initiate more than a bland, general response. Here again, temperament and personality are strong influences. Some, for example, find a continuing pleasure in observing the changing seasons as striking changes occur in the immediate landscape. A nearby field can be dense with foliage or starkly barren; it can be filled with the strong shadows of brilliant sun; or it might appear misty, foggy, the forms hardly visible. The total impact of the visual appearance, the contrast in line quality and tonal values, the patches of color, the mood, all stimulate ideas that can be translated into yarns and cloth.

The memory of certain colors seen fleetingly from a car window, a view of land patterns from a rising airplane, a deep look into a flower—all of these varying points of view can be brought into focus. They may be simplified if necessary, or developed into more complex arrangements appropriate to textile techniques. The beauty of rock formations, the graceful strength of birds, or the fantastic

**Figure 8.2**    An imprint of the grain on a slab of wood.

**Figure 8.3**    *Elusive Prey*    (14" x 22"), by Susan Oyler. Bold
stitching, beads, shells, and padding make strong textural contrasts
in this colorful panel.

forms of undersea life are all appealing in their own way to those with the interest and inclination for careful observation.

New buildings in construction as well as older structures call for a sensitivity to pattern formation, to contrasts of textural materials. Close examination should be made of building surfaces: brick, stone, and weathered wood, in addition to the ornamental details of various architectural styles.

The perceptive observer can see quite ordinary things from a fresh point of view. Fig. 8.3 on page 60, presents a formidable creature vainly trying to capture a beautiful "flying object." Is it lizard or dinosaur? The arrangement makes a quick answer difficult but it is really not important. This monster is of green felt cloth, slightly stuffed, and beyond the obvious stitches and bugle beads there is no attempt to disguise it. The colors are lively (see color plate, Fig. 8.3 on page 60) and the yarns used in a very direct, very honest way to convey this personal idea of a prehistoric terrain.

*Fly in the Ointment,* on page 63, brings into focus an unusual interplay of bold imagination with absolutely meticulous craftsmanship. The image is bizarre, with the fly magnified so that we can carefully examine the intricate details of its body structure. For the artist, the fascination of these details inspired a kind of thread-

**Figure 8.4**    Enlarged detail of the surface of a shell.

**Figure 8.5**    Detail study of a weathered barn door.

painting approach in the center portion of the design. Machine stitching with free movement of the cloth was worked in first, with a great deal of random overlapping. The fine hand stitching was then put in to accentuate the insect.

The panel is built up in a series of cloth layers, each serving as a frame for the center motif. Each layer, gradually increasing in size, is attached by hand in either a running stitch or a blind stitch. The

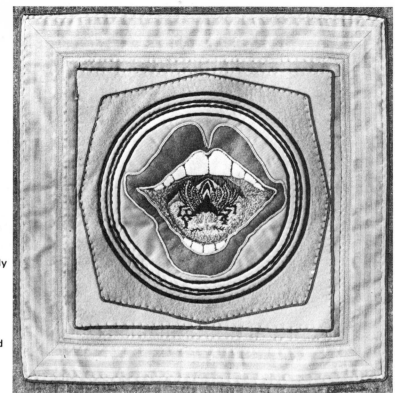

**Figure 8.6** *Fly in the Ointment* (19″ x 19″), by Joan Blumenbaum, is an appliqué panel built up with several layers of cloth. The hand and machine stitching in the center area is unusually detailed.

**Figure 8.7** Detail, *Fly in the Ointment.* The complexity of the hand stitching on the fly, surrounded by a background of freely overlapping machine embroidery and appliqué, is seen at close range.

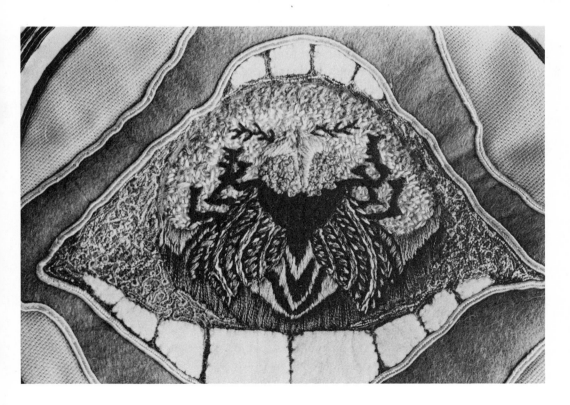

striking refinement of the technique, along with the incongruous subject matter, give this work a distinctive, highly individual quality.

*Landscape—Toward Spring* is an example of an idea that developed as a means of using yarns and cloth in almost a symbolic manner. Although there is no attempt at literal representation, the work is constructed in a way that suggests a changing landscape: the gradual giving way of snow and ice forms, the beginnings of plant growth in root structures, and, at the top, the emerging brightness of spring. The character of the yarns and cloth is used to signify the actual subtle changes that occur.

The upper section is of brown wool background with the appliqué shapes, also of wool, attached with handwork in straight stitching, using fine yarn in strong blues, greens, and purple. The lower portion is handwoven tapestry, attached to the background with hand stitching. The color is off-white in the side shapes and gray in the center. Linen yarn, in blue-green and green, was used to suggest the rootlike structures extending out from the ground. This idea evolved through very close study of the materials, especially the contrast achieved by combining the heavily textured surface of the woven section with the flat, though more brilliantly colored, upper portion of the design.

As some of the examples show, many ideas are developed by using different kinds of reference material. Details of bird and insect structure, wing patterns, and surface markings are best studied by consulting scientifically prepared encyclopedias. This is also true of skeletal forms and undersea organic life. Illustrated textbooks in botany and biology are valuable as sources of information on many kinds of natural forms, often with microscopic enlargements. These references, and many more, are available in libraries.

If available, a local historical museum or a museum of science or natural history is a source of ideas well worth seeking out. Artifacts and crafts from different cultures, in many materials, can stimulate thinking in the fibers medium. Exotic jewelry and metal filigree, pouches and beadwork of American Indians, useful objects decorated with distinctive patterns by primitive peoples: all of these things have a directness that is inspiring. Especially motivating are costumes from the past; these are full of intriguing details that can be given new interpretation in contemporary work.

It should be noted that many museums of this type often have much larger collections than they are able to display at any one time. Arrangements can usually be made through the curator's office to view this additional material, which often proves to be a storehouse of incredible diversity.

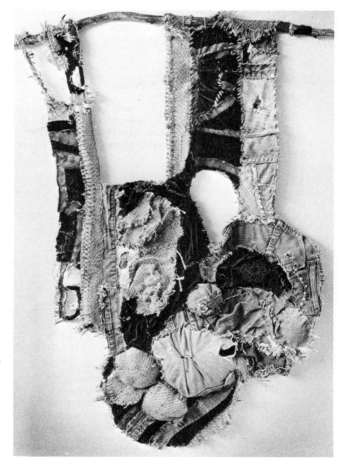

**Figure 8.8** *Landscape—Toward Spring* (50" x 20"), by the author brings together sections of handwoven cloth, loosley hanging linen yarn, stitching, and appliqué.

**Figure 8.9** A pair of old blue jeans, and a discarded sack of coarse burlap were cut up and reassembled by Patricia Kennedy to make this wall hanging mounted on a branch. Scraps of velvet introduce a contrasting element of luxury into this arrangement of appliqué, stitching, and padded forms.

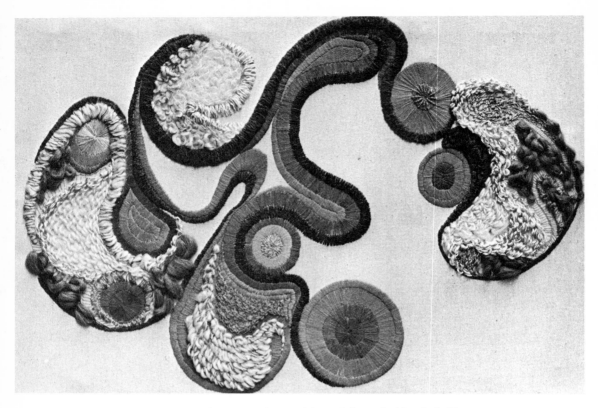

**Figure 8.10**   Simple forms, with carefully worked hand stitching in both coarse and fine yarns, convey a rhythmic pattern in this embroidered panel by Nancy Palladine. Osnaburg cloth was used as a background for the wool and synthetic yarns.

**Figure 8.11**   *Albatross Around the Neck*,   by Margaret Markle, was constructed with meticulous attention to detail. The material is soft white leather, stitched and lightly stuffed, with surface accents added with pen and ink and embroidery thread. The collar opens and closes so the piece can actually be worn.

**Figure 8.12** Studies of light and dark values made by enlarging details from black and white magazine photographs. These exercises help in refining an awareness of different kinds of shapes.

# **9** Sketching and Planning

The relationship of drawing and sketching to a medium in which yarns, threads, and cloth are used rather than pencils, pens, or brushes, should not seem ambiguous. There are many forms of drawing. The linear markings of yarns stitched into the surface of fabric are analogous to lines made on canvas or paper. Although the medium is different, the concern for line and the effects of line structures is similar.

Whenever the qualities of line are present in one's work, the process or activity that is called drawing is also present. Although drawing and sketching are fundamental, they need not be narrowly defined. When drawing, one begins to see and attempt to record certain aspects of the image. It is in no way a matter of duplicating what we see, but rather, of grasping some precise quality about the object or scene that we find intriguing or inspiring. The phrase "drawing turns the creative mind to expose its workings"* is a

*Edward Hill, *The Language of Drawing* (Englewood Cliffs, N.J.: Prentice-**68** Hall, Inc., 1966).

**Figure 9.1** *Who Am I? Where Am I
Going?* by Wanda von Weise. A pencil
drawing on white cotton is part of this
cloth form, appliquéd on batik, with
quilting.

poetic description of the real value of drawing as an important aspect
of imaginative thinking.

This attitude towards drawing has little to do with the "... but I
don't know how to draw" frustrations that frequently stand in the
way of making even a beginning. Rather, it is a way of recording
certain qualities that seem to be significant in viewing an object or
scene. What is it that we will want to remember later? What must be
searched out, observed, and noted down in some concrete way to
bring the essential aspects of the image back to mind? The answer
might be as simple as three lines capturing the movement of a bird
form or a detailed outlining of the tracery of a wrought iron gate.

Quite often, a simple drawing can initiate ideas that otherwise
might not come about. Making small collages from torn pieces of
magazine illustrations also can stimulate new ideas about shape and
color relationships. These experiences can be thought of as exercises
in planning for future work, helping to develop a confidence in
handling visual forms that can be translated into other materials.
Drawings, collages, and color sketches can also be valuable as points
of departure for working in the fibers medium. They should never be
literally copied, but used as a basis from which new patterns can
evolve.

Looking at much of the work illustrated, it is doubtful that these
completed examples could have been fully visualized in advance.
Whether in stitching or appliqué or a combination of techniques,
each piece was probably started and built up from a basic theme or
idea. Perhaps the idea was suggested initially by a drawing, a collage,
a photograph, or a memory of a scene once observed, or simply by a
grouping of particular yarns on some cloth. The first step is to
tentatively establish the idea in the medium with some blocking in of
stitches or placement of some cloth shapes. Then, the overall

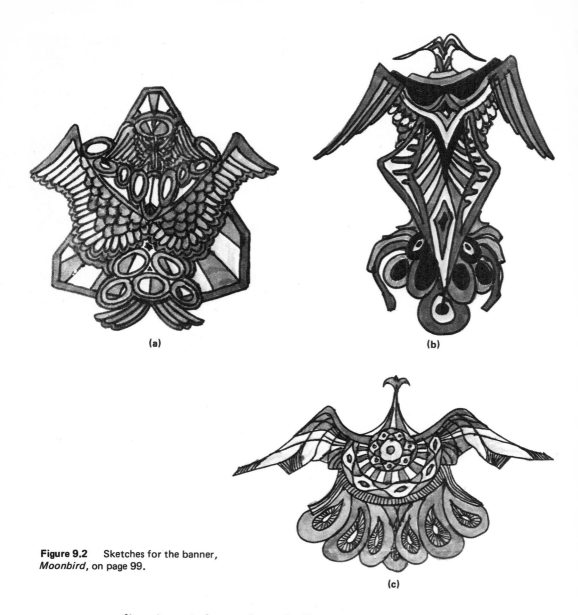

(a)

(b)

**Figure 9.2** Sketches for the banner, *Moonbird*, on page 99.

(c)

direction of the work gradually emerges; the design processes begin.

Many people, by nature or by training, prefer to work with a firmly established preliminary idea of at least the distribution of important shapes. Others are more comfortable working with only occasional brief references to a sketch, using it more as a guide in developing the overall mood rather than a strict layout of forms and colors. Those who claim that their work is never preplanned know that its direction and character are determined by what they have done before, by past experience with the medium and confidence in making new beginnings.

**70**

# 10 Color and Texture in Yarns and Cloth

## COLOR

In all visual art, color is a most persistent element. It catches the eye and draws the observer into the mood of the work. It is the element that communicates most directly, most personally. There are numerous theories about color, and a great deal of research has been done in the field, but color perception is not completely understood. For the artist and designer, it is the experience of working with color within the context of a particular medium which leads to the most valuable personal discoveries.

There is no doubt that an understanding of color is an important aspect of all work in stitching and appliqué methods. The ability to use color effectively depends initially on a highly attuned awareness of color itself. In our daily visual environment we rarely, if ever, see one color alone, isolated; we respond instead to color within a maze of other colors. This is true of our work. Each color we use functions as part of a totality of color, its placement and tonality modified by all the others. Judgments about color are always made in terms of other color.

**Figure 10.1**

The relation of various colors to human moods and human actions has long been studied. If we look carefully at colors in works of art, we become aware of a spectrum of feelings and attitudes that can be expressed. In the work shown in the color plates, the relationships of colors project many kinds of ideas. In some of the pieces the colors shout, in others they sing, or dance, or glow in the sun's warmth, or simply sit quietly and wait. It should be remembered that in this medium it is impossible to separate color from the tactile surface quality of the cloth or yarn. Thus, some colors seem to absorb the light, becoming deep and heavy, while others reflect it, appearing weightless and delicate.

There are no rules for using color; plans for color harmonies and guides for "correct" color usage that guarantee success should be regarded with suspicion. There is nothing intrinsically harmonious or unharmonious about any color or grouping of colors. These seemingly approved color schemes are usually a simple reflection of current trends or styles. We become accustomed to looking at certain colors used together and, by repetition, become conditioned into feeling that they are right. The validity of these combinations is transitory; they should never be considered easy solutions or inhibit individual color investigations.

It is sometimes thought that a proper solution to the problems of color selection implies working with only a few color variations, thus avoiding the risk of obviously discordant hues. However, if too few colors are used, the results can be lacking in interest and depth. In stitching, as well as in appliqué, the richness and warmth of the color

**Figure 10.2** *Arrangement* (32" x 24"), by Cheryl Bennett. The strong contrasts of oranges, golds, and black are seen in terms of value in this black and white photograph of a stitched panel.

come from a complexity rather than a paucity of tones. Even when the overall scheme is subdued, small areas of brilliant color bring out essential contrasts that give vitality to the total work. These bright accents may be minute in scale when compared to the larger, more dominant shapes, but they are, nevertheless, important.

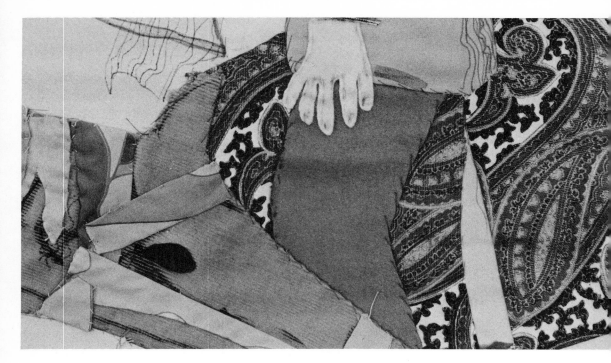

**Figure 10.3**    Brilliant colors in both plain and printed cloth are arranged in close proximity in this detail view of the wall mural on page 39.

The richest kind of color usage is very complex, made up of many different but closely interrelating hues. The familiar array of bright colors found on the standard color wheel can be changed, resulting in numerous variations in lightness, darkness, and intensity. To see this, the multicolored facets of nature can be studied to advantage; here, color distinctions are truly unlimited. It would be impossible to count the number of greens that can be found in a field of grass. The colors on wet stones are patches of a multitude of neutrals, strange mixtures of soft greens, purples, pinks, and browns. In natural forms, it is rare to find an evenly shaded area of color.

The initial steps toward a resourceful understanding of color begin with a more consciously directed awareness of coloration found everywhere. Outdoors, observe color in flowers, fields, rocks, and sky, the garments of people in crowds, building surfaces . . . in all of these we can sense the complexity of tonal and color relationships. Indoors, we are surrounded by different kinds of color, and can examine room interiors, bags of groceries, shelves of books, color cards in paint stores, photography in magazines, and, certainly, paintings in art galleries.

For the beginner, it is natural to begin to work with colors that one already likes and from this, learn to see the many variations

**74**    possible within each basic hue. Some experience with color mixing, using paints, will be helpful in understanding the different properties of color. For example, yellow, as a specific color or hue, cannot be produced by mixing and is called a primary color. Yellow can be mixed with other primary colors in differing amounts. When red is added, oranges are produced; the addition of blue results in a variety of greens.

When white or black is added to these colors, their value is changed and a range of pale tints and deep tones results. The brightness or intensity of the pure colors can also be changed by the addition of small amounts of other hues which are called complementary, since they are placed in opposite positions on the color wheel: for yellow, the complement is violet, for red—green, and for orange—blue. For work in textiles, it is not necessary to pursue color mixing with paints to scientific levels. Rather, it should be regarded as a means of observing at first hand how certain color variations are achieved, so that they can be recognized in yarns and cloth.

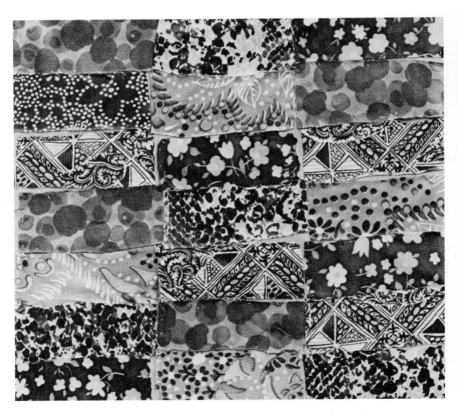

**Figure 10.4** The complexity of color interaction can be studied by arranging and observing pieces of patterned cloth in many varying colors.

**Figure 10.6** Neutral tones are well worth exploring for their subtlety and richness. This appliqué panel (24" x 36"), by Linda Murphy, uses cotton and rayon cloth in close grays, beiges, and black.

**Figure 10.5** Bands of striped cloth, each slightly different from the other, help to differentiate tone and color impact.

The diversity of color readily available in threads, yarns, and fabric is remarkable. Even a casual overview of yarn suppliers' sample cards or the lines of cloth bolts on fabric store counters give ample evidence of this. More careful study makes this tremendous variety even more apparent. There are literally hundreds of possibilities from which to select, ranging from pure, brilliant hues to soft and subtle tints and tones. In the instances where a particular color or range of colors cannot be found, it is possible to dye yarns and cloth for one's own use.

A collection of yarns and fabric in many different colors is necessary for anyone interested in textile work and ideal for direct experience in building color relationships in this medium. The collection should continually be expanded, with all kinds of small scraps brought together. Jumbled, improvised groupings can be made on different background tones. The same colors appear quite different when moved from a light to a medium to a dark ground.

These color workings cannot really be classified but are invaluable for developing a feeling for color and a confidence in putting different kinds of colors together. Vibrations, contrasts, and dissonants can be observed and mentally recorded, thus adding to the building of a personal and intuitive groundwork for color use.

## TEXTURE

The handling of threads, yarns, and cloth provides a direct encounter with texture, a response to the countless surface qualities sometimes apparent to the eye, but most distinctive when touched. The particular feel of a fiber substance or a type of cloth can be a means of identification and a guide to its appropriate use in designing.

As with color, the tactile sense grows and develops with continual observation and comparison of the great range of yarns and fabrics available. In this medium, texture cannot be separated from color, which affects the character of the surface at every turn. These are materials that must be handled if their unique tactile qualities are to be examined and compared. As was suggested for color study, a seemingly haphazard collection of scraps and pieces of many different surfaces in yarns, twines, cords, fringes, and cloth weaves will become an invaluable storehouse of opportunities for making textural judgments.

**Figure 10.7**    In this detail of a wall hanging by the author, many contrasting textural surfaces are evident: padded velvet, handwoven fabric, strands of yarn in bulk, and a wooden button.

The color/texture collection should contain as many varieties in yarns, threads, and fabric as it is possible to find. Most textile artists rarely abandon the role of selective scavenger and are constantly on the alert for new and intriguing "finds." The person getting started will find that friends and relatives who sew are an excellent source for small sections of fabric. Many seamstresses sense an intrinsic preciousness about cloth and cannot seem to throw leftovers away; there is often a bulging box of scraps in the closet or attic. This can be a beginning.

Browsing through rummage or discard shops will turn up wonderful old fabrics with coarse laces, fringes, braids, and intricate woven patterns, each with a different texture. Worn evening wear provides velvets, gauzy chiffons, and netting. To the discerning eye, quite ordinary things, such as mop heads, potato sacks, and cloth sausage

**Figure 10.8** Sections of handwoven cloth brought together for study, each with a different type of yarn and weave structure.

**Figure 10.9** Varying surfaces of cloth.

casings, have as much potential textural value as the rarer, more specialized laces and brocades.

The tactile qualities of yarns and cloth can best be observed by placing different kinds next to one another, so that contrasts become most obvious. In some types of fabric, the weave itself is very pronounced. This is especially true of coarser, more loosely structured cloth, such as burlap, coarse linen, coating woolens, and sisal sacking. Other kinds of cloth are woven very tightly, so that no indication of the character of the weave is evident on the surface.

Looking at groups of fabrics, each quite different in "feel" and

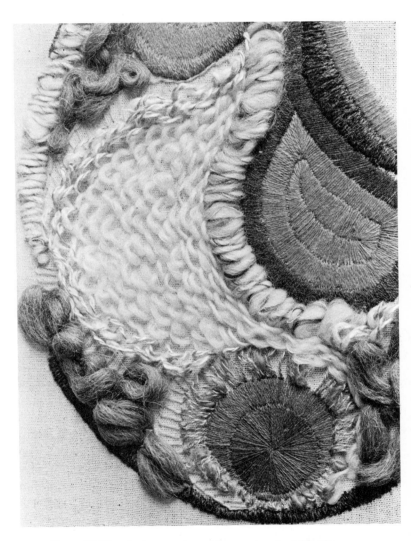

**Figure 10.10**   A close-up view of the panel on page 66. The beautiful variation in texture achieved by the yarns and stitches can be seen in sharp detail.

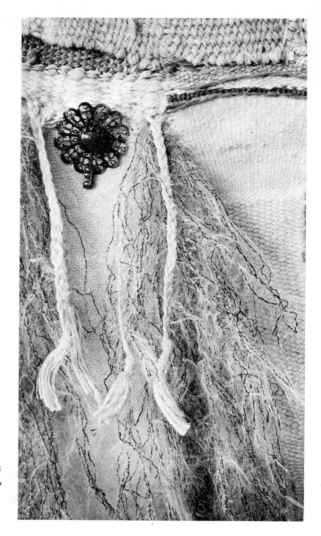

**Figure 10.11** Contrasting textures of woven wool, flowing gray mohair, and filigree belt buckle are seen at close range in this detail of the wall hanging on page 48.

weave structure, opens up ideas for experimentation in using varying textures together. This also helps in recognizing the intrinsic qualities of various types of cloth. Flannels are smooth, yet dense; they seem to absorb color. Felt, although nonwoven, is also smooth, flat, and seemingly porous. The shininess of satin, transparency of marquisette, open structure of netting, all of these varying surfaces can interact with one another, sometimes complementing, sometimes overpowering. Velvets, plushes, velours, and corduroy have a very pronounced depth of surface, while heavy braids, fringes, and manufactured furs produce extravagant relieflike effects.

There is enormous textural variation in yarns, which can be used to advantage in stitching and appliqué work. Uneven spinning produces slubbed effects, resulting in an overall thick and thin quality. Loops and knots can also be introduced into yarns during spinning. Some yarns have a crimped, curled appearance; others are soft and smooth, or furry, scratchy, or brittle. It is possible to work with fine strands of filament nylon or coarse Mexican wool, in addition to sleek metallic and plastic yarns.

Each bit of fabric or fiber substance has its own special tactile quality; each communicates in its own way.

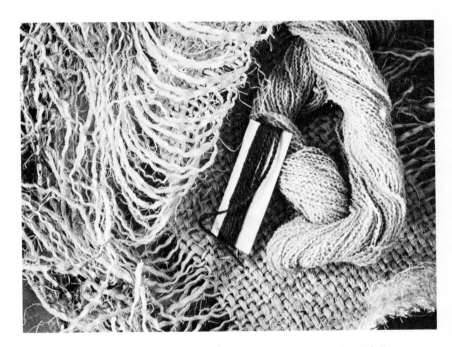

**Figure 10.12**    Sisal cloth, partially unravelled, is a background foil for softer yarns; judgments about combining textures can best be made from direct observation.

# 11 Using Found Material

When working in the various textile techniques, it often seems appropriate to incorporate materials other than those of a fibrous nature. The use of such objects as part of the design can provide ingenious textural accents and project a very lively, discerning attitude. Whatever the material, however, the boldness of its selection must be tempered by discretion in its use, so that there is a valid analogy or relationship between the object and the form of the textile. It should enhance rather than compete with the overall design of the work.

Small shells can be collected and successfully combined with stitching. Stones, dried plants, pieces of driftwood, and feathers of all sizes and colors are among other natural materials that can be considered appropriate for use in textile wall hangings and cloth constructions.

The search for manufactured materials can probably begin in one's own kitchen and basement, followed by trips to hardware stores,

**Figure 11.1**    Buttons, brooches, beads, and belt buckles form an
exotic mixture for reference and possible use in stitching and
appliqué work.

thrift shops, and the local five and dime store. It is possible to use
ordinary objects with great flair and imagination. Buttons of various
kinds, old jewelry, glass, mirrors, sequins, pearls, crushable foils,
beads, plastic, and leather have been used by textile artists. In
addition, metal screening, different types of wire, washers, and even
tin can lids are potentially useful.

It is possible to use these materials and objects for themselves,
allowing them to project a certain character or symbolic meaning.
Or, they can be used for their pattern or decorative value, thus losing
their original identity as they become a part of the other elements
within the design. Their selection and use should always be governed
by the mood and direction of the textile; nothing should be added at
random for the sake of putting in a bit of glitter.

Using found objects and materials can result in a fascinating
interplay with the yarns and cloth, evoking a rich or gaudy effect, a
nostalgia for a time long gone, or the reality of a blatant present.
Care is needed, however, because it is also possible to use these
materials in ways that are gross and inappropriate, betraying a lack of
judgment and sensibility. A discerning eye and a feeling for the visual
and tactile compatibility of material is required in both the selection
and use of these objects and "findings."

**Figure 11.2**    Detail of the textile panel described more fully on page 118. Dime-store pearls and jewelry, hat ribbons and laces add a regal touch.

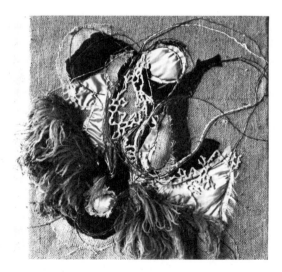

**Figure 11.3**    This mounted panel, by Carol Watson, uses ostrich feathers as part of the design, a compatible textural element with the stitching and appliqué cloth in velvet, satin, and cut lace. The background is burlap.

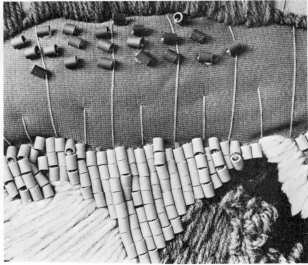

**Figure 11.4** These detailed photographs of the panel on page 60 show very clearly how the beading and the shell forms have been effectively integrated with the stitching.

**Figure 11.5** Detail showing feathers stitched onto the burlap background along with areas of stitching and hooking.

# 12 Stitching with Appliqué

In many of the textile wall hangings illustrated, more than one technique has been combined within the same piece. Stitching, related to appliqué sections used in a collagelike manner, has resulted in textural surfaces of great richness and subtlety. The effects have been described as "painterly," implying that there is no attempt to disguise the natural character of the cloth in any way.

Such qualities as frayed edges are frequently incorporated into the design without the restriction of turning under and hemming raw edges. Seemingly unrelated fabrics can be juxtaposed with flair and sensitivity, in ways that enhance contrasts in weight, surface, and color. Within a single piece, the techniques can vary greatly and range from an improvised spontaneity to areas requiring great discipline and control. Yet, like a complex collage painting, the interrelation of the different shapes, lines, and colors forms a coherent total arrangement within the overall space.

Working in this manner provides many opportunities for experimentation; it is an excellent approach for a beginner. The stitching can be purely functional, serving to hold the fragments and pieces of fabric in place, or it can provide interest in itself through the building

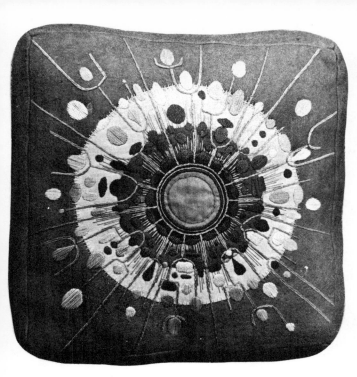

**Figure 12.1** *Pillow*, by Lynn Carver, is appliqué with stitching on orange felt.

**Figure 12.2** *Girl Talk* (22" x 22"), by Joan Blumembaum. Applied layers of cloth frame a contrasting circular shape in the center, the motif carefully worked in hand stitching.

**Figure 12.3** Detail of *Girl Talk*, showing the refinement of the carefully worked hand embroidery stitches.

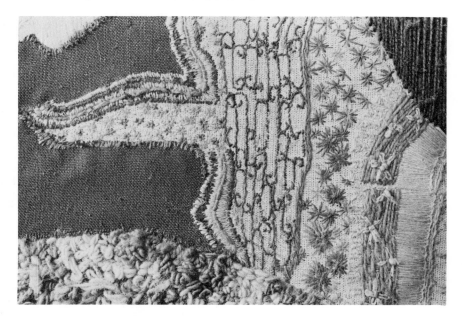

**Figure 12.4** Detail of panel on page 53. A close-up view of appliqué in plain cloth next to area of minute embroidery stitches.

**Figure 12.5** *This Is She* (24" x 30"), by Lucille Licata.
Appliqué cloth, slightly padded to suggest the forms of the figures,
is effectively combined with flat stitching to delineate shape
outlines. Both plain and printed fabrics were used in this mounted
panel on burlap background.

up of distinctive areas through overlapping. You can raise some
surfaces from the background if you partially stuff precut shapes of
cloth or introduce hooking and knotting techniques.

There are numerous possible approaches to using these techniques
together within the same work. In *Wall and Vine*, on page 29, both
stitching and appliqué are utilized, together with areas of hooking
and several padded smaller shapes. On a background of white wool,
appliqué shapes in off-white burlap and brown wool are attached
with stem stitching. Chain stitches were used to fill in the more
defined shapes.

**Figure 12.6**    Detail of
*This Is She*.    A felt-tip
pen was used to draw in
the features in each head.

For a more sculptural surface, several areas have been hooked; shorter, uncut loops are in the circular shapes and a long loop, cut afterward (see page 29), was used in the shaggy, more ruglike areas. The padding was done by partially stitching the outline of the shape, with an opening left so that the kapok could be stuffed in. Then the stitching was completed. The color effect is monochromatic, depending for contrast on the subtle gradations of the whites, off-whites, grays, and browns.

A very different frame of reference is seen in *Girl Talk*, shown on page 87. Stitching and appliqué techniques are again combined, but the subject matter is directly influenced by fashion photography. The result, however, is highly individualistic rather than illustrative. The figures are delineated in the most meticulous way using very tiny stitches worked with black thread.

The background for the stitched center section is heavy, white cotton, cut into a circular shape. Bias tape was carefully blind stitched around the rim of the circle, which was then mounted in appliqué fashion onto a square of velour, surrounded by an outer shape of striped denim. The initial impact is that of a framed painting, although there is no attempt to disguise the threads, stitches, and cloth.

Other examples show different approaches to combining these techniques. Printed or plain cloth can be used and the character of the stitching can vary from the bold, linear appearance, as seen in *This Is She*, to the very delicate, embroidery detail in the close-up view of *Girl Resting* (see page 88).

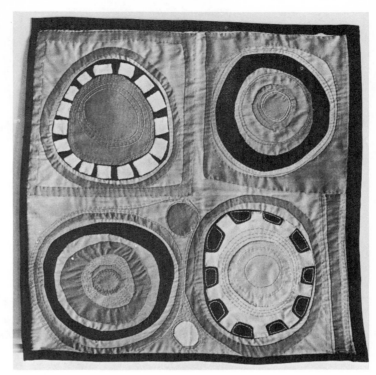

# 13 Appliqué Cutwork

Contemporary textile artists have responded to the surface cloth quality and primitive design motifs of the San Blas Island molas and find working in this technique a fascinating exercise in shape and color juxtaposition. If one understands the basic procedures involved, the technique is not difficult if it is handled on a small scale. It is time-consuming, however, if done in the traditional way with hand stitching used to hem the shape edges. The need for careful craftsmanship is an important consideration, since the effectiveness of the result is so dependent on refinement of detail.

Although this method of working with cloth has already been briefly described, more specific technical information might be helpful in getting started. In selecting fabric, medium-weight cottons (broadcloth, percale) or cotton-dacron blends are ideal, although soft woolens and even knits can be used.

Very rich color effects are obtained by choosing colors within a close range, such as red, orange, red-violet, and rust. More striking contrasts will result with more divergent colors such as red, yellow, and blue, each very bright. Many kinds of colors can be used together, but combinations of very intense colors with pastels should

**Figure 13.1**  *Four Circle Square*  (24" x 24"), by Carol
Schwartzott, is layered and cut appliqué. In addition to the
cutwork, applied shapes and surface stitching have also been used.

be avoided in this method. Contrasts that are too great cause
spottiness after cutting and destroy the overall coherency of the total
design. The colors should be studied carefully, placed next to one
another, before final selections are made.

Three or four pieces of cloth are needed, each the same size; these
are ironed and then stacked one directly over the other. For starting,
a practical size would be about 16 or 18 inches square or a
rectangular format of similar scale. Before cutting, the layers of
fabric are held together by several widely spaced rows of long basting
stitches. The design need not be completely worked out at the
beginning, since many ideas will occur as the work progresses. The
initial blocking in of the important shapes can be made on the top
layer, using white blackboard chalk (not prepared pastels) or a soft
pencil.

Using sharp, pointed scissors, cut into the cloth, following the
outline of the shape. Remember that the edge will be turned under
about a quarter of an inch for hemming, so allow for this when
cutting. One layer can be cut through, or several, depending on
which color is to be exposed. The edges will turn under for hemming
more easily if small cuts or clips are made along the rim of the shape.

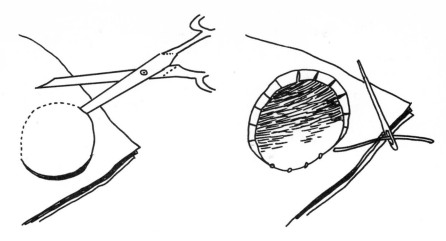

**Figure 13.2** Cutting and hemming for layered cutwork technique.

The blind stitch is usually used for the hemming, since it is hardly visible on the top surface. It is only necessary to turn under the top layer for hemming; therefore, when more than one layer is cut into, the edges of the cloth shapes underneath should be cut into more deeply.

As the work proceeds, the cloth will lose its flat appearance, gradually taking on a slightly padded surface because of the continual turning under of the shape edges before hemming. In designing, the most appropriate shapes are circular or have slightly rounded edges. Actually, any type of shape is possible, but the sharp angles of geometric figures are more difficult to handle.

All of the fabric scraps that are left after the cutting should be saved and possibly used as appliqué to add any shapes that are too small to cut away. Areas of appliquéd cloth can occur anywhere in the design. Surface stitching is also very effective and, if delicately worked, completely compatible with the cutwork technique.

In experimenting with this method, several variations are possible. Both plain and printed cloth can be used in the same piece, or each layer can be of a different printed fabric. Stripes, for example, in varying colors and widths can be used with this method, resulting in a very complex optical design effect.

The finishing can be done in several different ways. When all of the cutting and hemming is complete and the additional details in appliqué and stitching have been added, remove whatever remains of the basting stitches and iron gently. Do not expect the layers of cloth to retain their original alignment; retrimming will be necessary. The easiest way to finish the raw outside edges is to stitch on a wide (about two to three inches) strip of cloth, cut on the bias. It can be

**Figure 13.3** *Green Apples* (18" x 18"), also by Carol
Schwartzott, uses cotton fabric in blues and greens. The close
colors are visually effective, although the contrast is not apparent
in the black and white photograph.

of the same color as the top layer or, if contrast is wanted, one of the
other colors used in the design. This forms a border encasing the
edges and is hemmed on the reverse side.

For hanging, a rod can be inserted through several cloth loops
stitched to the top of the piece. Handled in this way, much of the
rod is exposed. The mounting rod can be completely hidden if a strip
of fabric is stitched to the top, forming a slot. A rod or dowel of
wood or metal can then be inserted.

This is a technique that can be enjoyed and explored as a direct
heritage of a thriving folk art tradition. The procedure can be
modified and adapted to be compatible with contemporary design
attitudes.

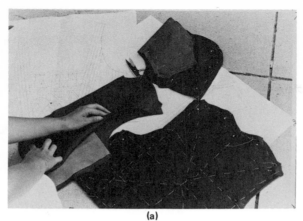

**(a)**

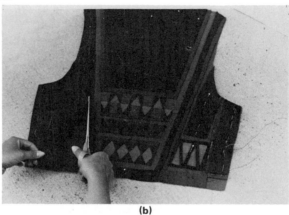

**(b)**

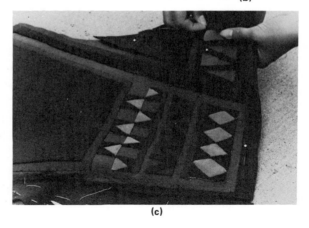

**(c)**

**Figure 13.4** (a, b, c) The preparation of a vest, in wool felt, in the
appliqué cutwork technique. (a) Placing the layers of cloth together
and holding them in place with rows of large basting stitches.
(b) Cutting sections out to expose the colors underneath.
(c) Stitching the layers together after the cutting has been completed.

# 14 Machine Stitching

The sewing machine has become an important asset to many textile artists since it can be used as a means of achieving a free type of "drawing" on the cloth. It can also provide an efficient aid in attaching sections of applied cloth to backgrounds. Unusual versatility in stitching can be achieved with the machine if the presser foot and feeder action are removed according to appropriate model directions.

With a darning foot inserted in place of the normal presser foot and the feeder teeth lowered or covered with a metal plate, the direction and continuity of the stitching can be guided with little difficulty as the cloth moves freely under the needle. All manner of linear effects can be achieved with straight stitching and the range of possibilities is even further enlarged by using zigzag stitches. Either the straight stitch or the zigzag stitch can be worked directly on a single layer of fabric or used for attaching applied sections to the background cloth. In addition, the sewing machine is appropriate for stitching on multilayered fabrics for quilting or stuffing techniques.

The possibilities in using the sewing machine become evident with

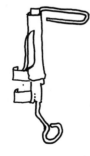

**Figure 14.1**
Darning foot which will fit most standard model machines.

96

some experimentation on small pieces of cloth. For the beginner, practice is essential for gaining an understanding of the actual use of the machine as well as becoming familiar with the numerous variations in stitching that can be achieved. The important technical aspects of the machine to be explored are both straight and zigzag stitching with free movement of the cloth for embroidery effects in surface stitching and for attaching applied sections of cloth to backgrounds.

## FREE SURFACE STITCHING

With the machine set for straight stitching (this procedure can be used for older machines that do not have the zigzag attachment), the feeder teeth are lowered or covered with a metal plate, depending on the make of the machine. The presser foot normally used is removed

**Figure 14.2** Square and rectangular sections of both plain and printed fabric were pieced by Sue Katz in making this skirt. The stitching was done on the machine.

and in its place a darning foot is inserted. This is a special foot that operates on a spring action, holding the cloth lightly in place during stitching. On straight-needle machines, standardized models of the darning foot are interchangeable. The machine should be correctly threaded, as for ordinary sewing, with tensions fairly loose.

With the machine set up in this way, both hands can be used to guide the cloth in all different directions—forward, backward, or side to side, making straight lines, curves, or circles. When lines of stitching are worked in close rows, shape areas can be suggested. Different textural surfaces can be obtained by controlling the spacing of the rows of stitchings and by overlapping stitches in different directions.

The stitch length is no longer controlled by the lever on the machine. If the fabric is moved about quickly with the machine running at a moderate speed, the stitches will be long. Short stitches will result if the cloth is moved slowly under the needle. Machine speed is really of no advantage in this type of work; the richest effects are built up slowly and carefully with numerous short stitches.

Practice experiments should be tried on different weights of cloth, ranging from heavy felt to sheer organdy. While the use of the darning foot makes it possible to efficiently guide and control all weights of fabric in free surface stitching, some craftsmen prefer to use a small embroidery hoop to hold the cloth. With this method, the fabric section to be stitched is tautly stretched in the hoop and one side of the hoop placed under the needle.

Although there is no presser foot on the machine when the hoop is used, the lever must be in the down position. During the stitching, the hoop is guided with the hands and then moved about to new sections of the cloth as each area is completed. When you are using the hoop, it is important to stretch the cloth as tightly as possible. Otherwise, puckering will occur and control will be difficult. Be sure the needle is at its highest point when placing the rim of the hoop under it to avoid accidentally breaking or bending it. While the hoop can be used successfully, the darning foot is much easier to use and allows for much greater control.

After completing several small samples using straight stitching to achieve embroidery type effects, try some additional experiments using the zigzag stitch. The procedure is the same, except that the width of the stitch can be adjusted. As with straight stitching, the spacing of the stitches depends on how slowly or rapidly the cloth is moved under the needle. When wide zigzag stitches are closely aligned, shape areas fill in rapidly. For additional interest, change

**Figure 14.3** Detail of the felt banner, *African Theme*, on page 111. The shapes were cut out of felt and attached to the felt background with straight machine stitching, about 1/8″ from the edge.

**Figure 14.4**   Detail of *Moonbird.*   The character of the machine stitching over the corduroy is very clearly seen.

**Figure 14.5**   *Moonbird*   (47" x 41"), by Valerie Bautz, was made entirely of corduroy in brilliant blues and reds. Close, zigzag machine stitching in black attaches the cloth to the background and covers the raw shape edges.

thread colors frequently and allow rows of stitches to partially overlap. Keep the practice samples as references for future work.

## MACHINE STITCHING IN APPLIQUÉ

The method of using the machine with the movement of the cloth guided by hand is applicable to both surface stitching and appliqué work. Smaller pieces of cloth can easily be attached to backgrounds with either free straight or zigzag stitches. As the illustration shows, the stitches are not simply functional; they provide a very definite design element and form a transition between the background and the

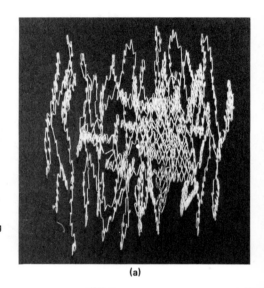

**Figure 14.6**   Samples of machine stitching made with the feeder teeth lowered and a darning foot inserted in place of the regular presser foot.
a. random zigzag stitching
b. attaching appliqué cloth with zigzag and straight stitching
c. zigzag stitching around an opening cut into the cloth

(a)

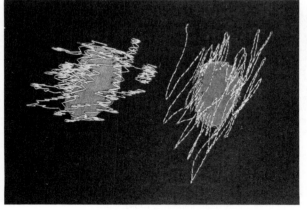

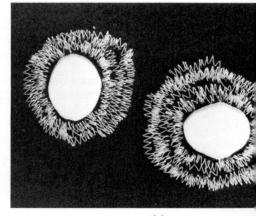

(b)

(c)

applied cloth. The rows of stitches, in this case, do not clearly outline the shape of the applied fabric. When the stitches freely overlap, the new cloth becomes an integral part of the background.

In different types of work such as large banners and wall hangings, the appliqué technique is emphasized to a far greater degree and the stitching is of less importance as an element in the design. The dominant interest is in the variation in shape and color of the applied areas of cloth. The stitching is necessary primarily for its functional value in firmly attaching one fabric to another. Although any type of surface stitching affects the overall character of the design, the shape outlines are of major importance.

**Figure 14.7**  *Greenbird,*  by Jan Peterson, uses both machine and hand stitching to form the lightly padded body form the lightly padded body form of cotton with the feet constructed of felt.

For these textiles, the machine is set up as it would be for normal sewing, with the feeder teeth up and the presser foot down. Here again, both straight stitching and zigzag stitching are appropriate, with the choice made on the basis of the type of cloth used and the kind of surface stitch most consistent with the total design.

A necessary consideration here is whether the cut cloth shapes will ravel if the edges are not completely turned under or covered with stitches. Often, on smaller pieces done primarily with hand stitching, exposed frayed edges of applied shapes are very much in character with the overall feeling of the design. However, on larger pieces, especially appliqué banners and wall hangings, or quilt tops that will be subjected to wear, the craftsmanship suffers if the edges are not cleanly finished.

Straight machine stitching can be used in appliqué work when the fabric selected for cutting does not ravel. Felt, for example, is an ideal choice for applied shapes of different sizes and colors. The background can be of the same material or of any sturdy fabric compatible with felt, such as heavyweight wool, cotton duck, osnaburg, or hopsacking. After cutting, the shapes of the felt are pinned or basted onto the background with the stitching running about $\frac{1}{8}$ to $\frac{1}{16}$ inch from the edges.

When fabrics are used that fray easily when cut, such as light- and medium-weight cottons and rayons, the zigzag stitch can be used to attach the applied shapes to the background. Zigzag stitching is much wider and therefore much more prominent than the straight stitch, resulting in a very strong outline of the shape. Since the stitches are usually very closely aligned, an important consideration is the choice of thread color. Small trial samples are the most practical guides for making these judgments.

## CUTWORK METHODS

The textile methods involving cutwork, described on page 93, can also be done on the sewing machine. Here, several layers of cloth are placed over each other with the design image formed by cutting away sections of the upper layers, exposing the different colors underneath. Initially, the procedure is very much the same as that for hand sewing. Large hand-basting stitches, in widely spaced rows, hold the three or four layers of fabric in place.

At this stage, a procedure slightly different from that used with

**Figure 14.8** Detail of the banner, *Cycle*, on page 112. Machine stitching is seen on the wing form and on the border decoration.

hand sewing can be followed. All of the important shape areas in the design are lightly sketched on the top layer with pencil or fine chalk. With the machine set for a narrow but widely spaced zigzag stitch, work around the outline of each shape. For this, the presser foot is down and the feeder teeth up.

After all of the shape areas in the design have been outlined, begin cutting, going through as many layers as necessary to expose the required color. When the cutting is completed, stitch around each shape again with a wider, closely set zigzag stitch that will completely cover any exposed raw edges. Both plain and printed fabrics can be used and thread color can be changed at any time. It is also possible to add additional stitching, in the free embroidery method, within the shapes.

**Figure 14.9**    Close zigzag machine stitching is used to attach the appliqué shapes to the background in this detail of a commercially made banner designed to advertise a product.

## OTHER POSSIBILITIES

Holes of different sizes and shapes can be cut out of a piece of cloth. With the machine set for free movement of the cloth, rows of straight stitches can be worked over the openings, going back and forth and from side to side. Within the open area, an uneven lacelike network of delicate lines will result.

Another variation is to remove sections of warp or filler rows from a loosely woven background material. The remaining threads will be in one direction only within that area. Use the zigzag stitch and move the fabric freely; groups of these remaining threads can then be secured and interlaced in a random way. With overstitching and continual change in direction, numerous textural effects can be created.

The sewing machine can also be used to advantage in patchwork, quilting, and trapunto techniques. Large pieces of cloth can best be handled in the machine if you roll up each side, exposing only the area being worked on at the time. Fit one of the rolled ends under the arm opening of the machine; the other rests on the table surface to the left of the needle.

**Figure 14.10** *Album Cover*,
by Lenore Davis. Machine quilting
was used to form this velvet cover,
which flips over, as a book.

**Figure 14.11** *Unity In Three* (23" x 23"), by Joan
Blumenbaum, shows a mastery of sewing machine techniques,
as well as hand stitching, in building this layered cloth panel.

From the illustrations, it is evident that the sewing machine is valuable for purely functional reasons, as a time-saving device, or because it can contribute particular effects and unique qualities that cannot be obtained by hand methods. Combinations of hand and machine work, within the same piece, are also very effective and should be continually explored. Learning to use the machine creatively can be the beginning of visualizing new ideas that can lead to new ways of working.

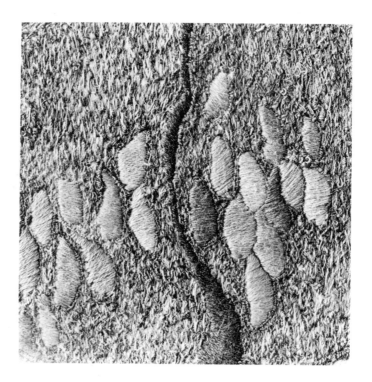

**Figure 14.12** Detail, *Unity In Three.* Hand stitching delineates the stem and seeds of the apple, over a maze of highly textured machine stitching, worked with very loose bobbin tension.

# 15 Banners

The new prominence of the banner type of cloth wall hangings brings about a natural appreciation for the lively flags, signs, and pennants that were so much a part of past cultures. All of the strong color and vitality of a medieval tournament seem to be reflected in contemporary textile banners as they bring together the spirit of traditional methods of working with present-day design ideas and imagery.

The pennant or sign made of cloth was probably first used as a means of designating authority or aristocratic office. Although the exact origins are not known, wood and metal standards carrying a sign or symbol were used by the ancient Egyptians. As time went on, this method of designating rank or station expanded into the more generalized function of identification for groups having a unified interest or allegiance.

The Roman legions carried emblems to their battlefields and centuries later, the Crusader armies of Europe displayed their own flags and banners. Tracing the history of flags alone becomes a fascinating worldwide excursion into the politics and attitudes of many different countries. From its earliest history, the Church used

**Figure 15.1** Banner by Norman LaLiberté. See pages 109-110 for more examples on the same theme.

textile banners in ceremonial pageantry. With the growing interest in heraldry in medieval Europe, symbolic cloth banners were displayed to great advantage in tournaments and festivals.

With the industrial age, this art form was largely forgotten. It has only been within recent years that large banners and cloth wall hangings have been widely accepted by architects as a warm and humanizing addition to walls and space areas in contemporary buildings. Impressive in size and brilliant in color impact, these works are a much needed enrichment to present-day interiors.

The cloth banners of Norman LaLiberté have been most influential in inspiring other textile artists. They are monumental in size and unique in their bold use of color and symbolic design elements. With a personal imagery evolving from a deep interest in symbols, his banners are peopled with figures reminiscent of ages past. Baroque saints and angels, Victorian ornaments, strange mythological animal

(a)

**Figure 15.2** Banners by Norman
LaLiberté, part of a series of eight,
designed on the theme of the
Evolution of the Great Seal of New
York. (Courtesy, James Stewart Polshek
and Associates, Architects.)

(b)

**Figure 15.2**   (cont.)

(c)

creatures, along with doves and garden flowers, all are arranged and stitched in place.

In these banners, the shape motifs are simplified and so are perfectly suited to the appliqué technique. The stitching is done primarily with the zigzag sewing machine, attaching and outlining the sections of cloth, bits of brocades, tassels, and fringes. Whether the themes are religious, historical, or humorous, these banners project an imaginative turn of mind.

Banners by other artists reflect many varying ideas about subject-matter inspiration and use of materials. As an example, the banner-type wall hanging, *African Theme*, was inspired by the geometric forms of Ethiopian calligraphy. The artist found the letter shapes appealing as the basis for a design arrangement and, because of their simplicity, most appropriate for using straight machine stitching on wool felt. The specific words selected for the design say "I love you" in Ethiopian.

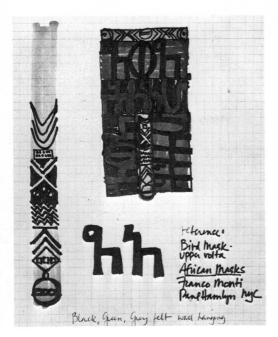

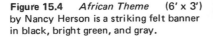

**Figure 15.3**  Preliminary sketches for the banner, *African Theme.*

**Figure 15.4**  *African Theme*  (6' x 3') by Nancy Herson is a striking felt banner in black, bright green, and gray.

Black and bright green were chosen for the important color areas, with a light gray background used for the band at the top and the center portion. These three colors are sufficient because the boldness of the shapes results in a visual arrangement of very strong contrasts. Tribal mask motifs were used as the basis for the design on the top and center section, with the smaller pieces of black felt attached to the gray background using machine stitching.

The sketches show how the plan of the banner evolved and give an excellent indication of the artist's thoughts. The overall arrangement was changed several times until the final and most satisfactory sketch came about. Since banners are so large, planning is best done to scale so that proportions will be the same. Working on lined graph paper, as was done here, is a practical solution to the problem of enlarging the shapes properly later.

Religious banners are again becoming an important aspect of today's church architecture, adding a lively accent of brilliant color and strong, symbolic design elements. Sometimes the interpretation is abstract; at other times, a distinctive Byzantine or primitive influence is apparent. Regardless, these works are a welcome addition, providing an enrichment to the building and a visual treat for the viewer.

**Figure 15.5** *Angels of the Lord*, by Sister Helena Steffens-meier, is an ecclesiastical banner worked entirely in hand embroidery stitches.

**Figure 15.6** *Cycle* (26" x 50"), by Joan Lenz, is a banner wall hanging designed with flat appliqué shapes and especially constructed relief forms that extend from the background.

Many contemporary church banners, ark curtains, or dossal hangings use machine stitching as a more efficient and less tedious method of working on large pieces. *Angels of the Lord*, see above, is different in that it is done entirely in hand embroidery. Open chain stitching, the cross stitch, straight stitch, and French knots can easily be recognized within the different areas of the work. Several variations of these basic stitches are included.

The forms have been simplified into an arrangement of shapes. The major interest is in the color and the textural variation achieved by the use of the different types of stitches. The six angel figures are placed next to one another in a manner reminiscent of figures in a Byzantine mosaic. Although religious in subject matter, this banner is not meant to be profound. It has a direct and primitive appeal, with the angels forming a serene, unpretentious group.

The banner, *Cycle*, also uses Biblical symbols. It, too, has a strong primitive quality but is unusually complex technically, in that several different methods of appliqué and relief cloth construction are combined. As a result, the work has both flat and sculptural areas forming a striking interplay between the raised and background sections. The background is a heavy purple cotton, with brilliant pink velveteen used for the angel figures and in the flame shape. Blue cotton is used for the wave sections in the lower portion.

Many of the appliqué shapes are attached with close zigzag machine stitching, although handstitching was used in the vertical center stripe. Machine embroidery, with free movement of the cloth, can be seen on the garment borders of the figures. While one of the angel's wings is stitched down completely, the other is constructed so that it actually projects from the background. This padded three-dimensional form is embellished with machine stitching (detail view on page 103) so that a well-defined relief surface is created.

The wave forms at the bottom of the design were also constructed to project from the background. The scalloplike top of each section was stitched separately about a quarter-inch from the edge; then it was stuffed with dacron filler, and tacked to the background at the lower edge. The refined sense of craftsmanship, in spite of the involved technical procedures, is very evident in the final result. Imagination, and a very personal way of utilizing material, make this banner an outstanding achievement.

**Figure 15.7**   A patchwork square, made up of smaller squares of printed cloth, before quilting.

**Figure 15.8**   Contemporary patchwork quilt by Ann Bryant.

# 16 Quilting and Sectional Padding

Quilting, trapunto, and other types of sectional padding are used effectively and with great innovation in contemporary work. Quilting, especially, is another of the older textile techniques that offers inspiration to today's artists as a means of achieving many kinds of relief effects and surface variations.

Known for centuries in Europe, quilting became enormously popular with the early American settlers. The designs were worked out by women with no formal training, using odd bits of leftover cloth, yet many are remarkable for their lively visual effects. Large quilts were very time-consuming, with all of the work done completely by hand. They were frequently made by groups to break the monotony; these "quilting bees" combined the enjoyment of a social gathering with the sharing of pride in the completed piece.

In traditional quilting, a soft but springy padding is placed between the top and bottom layers of fabric. The top layer of cloth is embellished in some way, either by appliqué or patchwork, with the bottom layer usually serving as a plain backing. The stitching goes through the three layers of material. When done by hand, a

**Figure 16.1** *Moonscape*
(42" x 30"), by Pamela Reed,
is designed with areas of
sectional stuffing on an open
canvas mesh background. The
exposed yarns are white, with
unbleached muslin used for the
relief forms.

running stitch is used. Most large-scale quilting today, however, is
done with the sewing machine.

Sections of cloth that are stuffed or padded to form relief shapes
against a flat background are not difficult, technically, and can add
greatly to the character and dimension of the work. The manner in
which these techniques are incorporated into the total design will
naturally vary, depending on the nature of the image and the
expressive intent of the artist. As the illustrated work shows, the
raised areas can be very subtle, even partially hidden within a maze
of yarns and stitches, or very pronounced, becoming the focal point
of the design.

Trapunto is a type of quilting in which only certain sections of the
design are raised. It differs from standard quilting in that two layers
of cloth, rather than three, are used in the stitching. Often the top
layer of fabric is somewhat more stretchable than the bottom, but
this is not always possible because of design requirements. For wall
hangings, the bottom layer can be considered a backing. If the piece
is to be finished in a three-dimensional manner, however, the same
fabric can be used for both top and bottom layers.

The design is stitched into the two layers of cloth either by hand
or machine. This is a technique that is ideally suited to machine
stitching. Geometric shapes or those with widely curving lines can be
done with the machine set in the usual way. Smaller, more complex

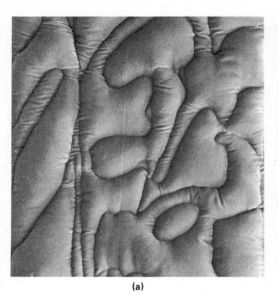
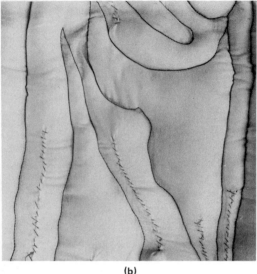

(a) (b)

**Figure 16.2**    Front and back details of trapunto stuffing.

shapes can be stitched more efficiently with the darning foot in place of the presser foot, the feeder teeth down and the cloth moving freely under the needle.

Any shape that is stitched completely around can be stuffed with kapok or similar material. A small slit is cut into the backing fabric on the reverse side, and the appropriate amount of stuffing is pushed into the opening with a knitting needle or any other suitable stick. When a sufficient amount of stuffing has been inserted, the shape will form a well-defined raised area. The slit opening can then be stitched closed by hand.

On three-dimensional pieces, the stitching and stuffing are done concurrently. Since slit openings are not wanted, each shape is stitched and stuffed, one at a time. Before the stitching around each shape is completed, a small opening is left through which the stuffing material can be pushed. Then the stitching continues, closing the gap and completing the outline of the shape. With very small shapes, the final, closing stitches can be done by hand.

The work illustrated shows several different approaches to the use of trapunto and related stuffing techniques. The variations in the final results emphasize the flexibility of these methods; according to the way they are handled, they can be adapted to many different kinds of ideas. In most of the examples shown, the stuffed sections are combined with flat stitching, appliqué, and in some cases, **116** hooking. The fabrics used range from muslin to velvet to burlap.

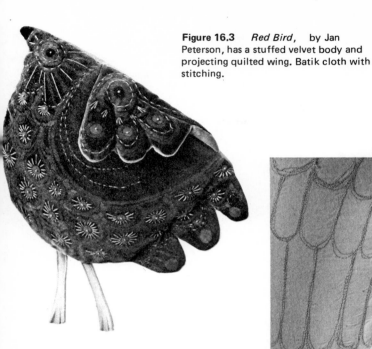

Figure 16.3 *Red Bird*, by Jan Peterson, has a stuffed velvet body and projecting quilted wing. Batik cloth with stitching.

Figure 16.4 Detail, *White Angel*. The qualities of line drawing achieved with machine stitching are evident in this close-up view.

In the panel, *White Angel*, (see above) machine stitching plays an important part in delineating the character of the central figure and the surrounding wing and arch form. With the machine set for free movement of the cloth (described on pages 97-100), both the running straight stitch and the zigzag stitch were used, detailing the rhythmic elements in the design with a smooth continuity.

Unbleached cotton muslin was selected for both the top and bottom layers. The stitching detailing the head and garment of the figure was done on one layer only, as was the detail work on the

**Figure 16.5** *White Angel* (20" x 48"), by Joyce Lenz, shows complex machine stitching and trapunto stuffing on a background of unbleached muslin.

**Figure 16.6** This interpretation of *Elizabeth R* (30" x 50"), by Elizabeth Deare, effectively combines several textile techniques, as well as different fabric textures.

**118**

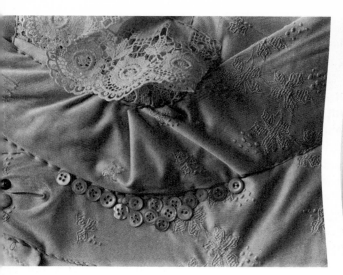

**Figure 16.7**    Detail of *White Gloves.*

**Figure 16.8**    *White Gloves*    (36" x 18"), by Diane King. The stuffed gloves, fan, and doily convey an eerie and somewhat nostalgic mood.

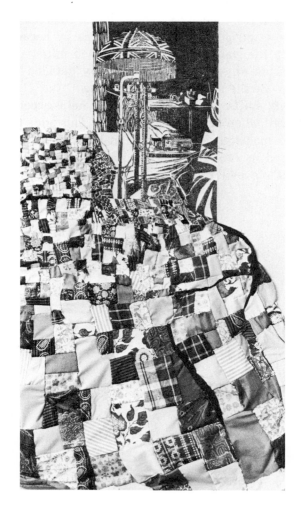

**Figure 16.9**    *Interior With Quilt*    (32" x 20"), by Linda Lee. The quilt shown in the corner of the block print is expanded onto the background in actual cloth patchwork.

arch. Then, with the two layers together, the rest of the stitching was completed. The figure and arch form were stuffed by the insertion of dacron fiber filling through a small slit in the backing.

A very different figure interpretation, also in neutral tones and utilizing the trapunto technique, is *Elizabeth R*, on page 118. Here also, both the top and bottom layers of fabric are unbleached muslin, the stuffed areas primarily in the skirt and bodice. The sleeves and hands were constructed as separate forms and stitched on later, with partial stuffing in the hands. Both hand and machine stitching were necessary.

Different types of cloth were used for the cloak and sleeves, with a stiff lace collar framing the face. The face is especially interesting, formed as a masklike appliqué piece, with hand stitching and partial stuffing. Many found objects, bits of discarded jewelry, beads, and ribbons contribute to the overall image.

*White Gloves*, on page 119, successfully organizes stuffed forms and is an excellent example of the use of commonplace objects as a means of symbolizing ideas. The long, white gloves, first seen on a rummage counter, were intriguing to the artist primarily because of their associations with the glamour of a past era. Their initial appeal, both as once-fashionable objects and as beautifully detailed cloth, was sufficient to motivate the beginnings of this panel.

The idea of partially stuffing some of the gloves helps accentuate the forms as they were when actually being worn. This adds to the symbolic quality and makes a richly dimensional arrangement. The other objects included—a lace doily, a fan, and a series of tiny buttons—all enhance the overall mood.

# 17 Printed and Dyed Backgrounds

Any hand-printed or dyed cloth can be used as a background for further work with either hand or machine stitching. Such fabrics can also be used in many of the appliqué methods, the printed and dyed images resulting in unusual diversity in color and pattern juxtaposition. Commercially printed materials have been used creatively when combined with other textile methods.

Since the stitching or appliqué techniques are emphasized, a complete mastery of the printing or dyeing procedures is not required. A basic familiarity with the important procedural steps is necessary, however, for appropriate planning. The information given here will provide a brief description of the different methods and show specific examples of their application. For more detailed technical directions, several excellent books listed in the bibliography are suggested.

With cut blocks of wood or linoleum, imprints can be made on cloth, creating designs that are often suitable for additional work with stitchery or appliqué. The printing can be done on almost any type of fabric, either opaque or transparent, with the block treated as a single motif or part of a repeat format. In either case, whatever is added by incorporating other techniques should enlarge the central

**Figure 17.1** *Gothic Facade* (28" x 18"), by Jeffrey Smith. This linoleum block was printed on several different background colors, then cut up and reassembled as appliqué sections.

idea and not simply decorate the printed image. For technical information on block printing and other methods of relief printing see *Design on Fabric* by Meda Johnson and Glen Kaufman.

In *Interior with Quilt,* on page 119, the cut linoleum block was printed in the upper-center section of the background cloth, in this case, osnaburg. The fabric is a coarse cotton, off-white, receptive to the block printing ink and easily stitched into with a needle. The size of the finished panel is 22" × 34".

The subject matter of the print is an arrangement of familiar objects in a room interior, designed in a representational manner. In the foreground, a portion of a quilt is seen. As the idea took form, the quilt was extended in cloth past the original boundary of the print, filling the remaining lower section of the background fabric. The patchwork technique was used to build the small areas of plain and printed cotton scraps that were appliquéd to the background. In the color plate, the contrast of the dark, flat printed image and the multicolor partial relief of the patchwork are an unusually effective combination.

In the appliqué panel, *Gothic Facade,* on page 122, there is a somewhat different application of linoleum block printing. Here, the imprint (about 8" × 15") was made in black ink on six pieces of cotton sailcloth, each a different and very bright color. When the prints dried, they were cut up and then reassembled as appliqué sections joined in different ways. The size of the original printed image expanded, and a mosaiclike pattern effect is conveyed through the arrangement of colorful sections of imprinted architectural details.

Each of the cut pieces was attached to the background with straight stitching done on the sewing machine. The edges were turned under about ½" to prevent fraying, with each shape pinned in place before stitching. In several areas, hand embroidery stitching adds additional detail.

## BATIK

Batik is an ancient method of resist dyeing on cloth. First, hot wax is brushed onto the fabric, establishing the basic shapes in the design. Then dyes are applied, either by sectional brushing or by the entire cloth being dipped into a cool dyebath. When the piece is dry, additional wax is applied to cover areas of color to be retained in the design. This is followed by further dyeing, in different colors. Successive wax and dye applications continue until the design is

**Figure 17.2** In this panel by Jan Peterson, batik, appliqué, and stitching techniques are combined.

complete. All of the wax is then removed and the design is permanently dyed into the fabric.

The small panel (18″ × 18″) on this page shows the batik process combined with both stitching and appliqué. The outer circular motif was dyed into the cloth with the batik method. In the center, a shape of cut felt is attached to the background with a small running stitch. Fine embroidery thread was used for the additional hand stitching, which accents the shapes.

*Dream Landscape*, the wall hanging on page 125, is larger (52″ × 32″) and somewhat more complex. Here, a completed batik cloth was cut up into sections which were used as appliqué on a background of natural linen. Hand stitching, primarily the stem stitch and chain stitch, serves as a transition between the batik-dyed shapes of fabric and the linen background.

**Figure 17.3**    *Dream Landscape*    (52" x 32"), by the author is an example of batik cloth sections used as appliqué and combined with stitching.

## TIE DYE

Figured cloth obtained by any of the tie-dye resist methods can also be further embellished with stitching. The shapes in the design should not be overly complex so that the applied stitching is important for its own surface quality, truly strengthening the image rather than becoming a superfluous addition.

The wall panel, *Growth*, on page 126, is an example of the tie and dye technique used initially on the background fabric. The character

**Figure 17.4**    Detail showing tie-dyed cloth used as partially stuffed sppliqué, surrounded by hooking and stitching.

**Figure 17.5**    *Growth*    (28" x 36"), by Carol Giulianelli. Tie-dye work, before the stitching, provided the varied background colors in this wall hanging.

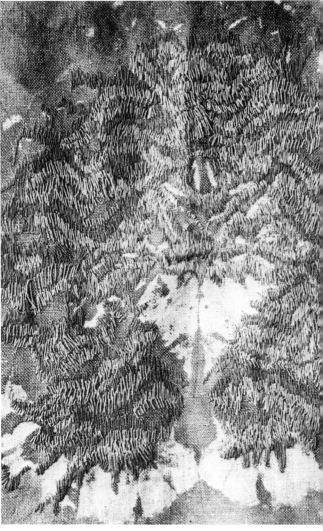

of the resulting shapes then suggested the direction of the additional work in hand stitching.

Natural burlap was used as the background fabric. With the cloth folded in half, several large folds were made along the center and securely tied. The first bath was a bleach solution, resulting in the light areas. After rinsing, additional folds were placed in different areas, tied, and then dyed in red on one side of the tie and purple on the other.

The stitching does not add radically new design elements but rather enriches the forms already dyed into the cloth. Although the colors vary, only the straight stitch is used. The techniques of batik and tie dye utilized in these illustrations are described in detail in *Designing in Batik and Tie Dye* by Nancy Belfer.

## SILK-SCREEN PRINTING

A familiarity with simple silk-screen printing methods can provide excellent starting points for developing ideas that can be further related to work with stitching and appliqué. This is a versatile

**Figure 17.6**    A silk-screen print, in white ink, formed the basic pattern shapes, before stitching. Designed by Carol Schwartzott.

medium; it is possible to obtain a great range of visual effects, from bold to delicate, linear to massive, as well as numerous combinations achieved by overprinting.

In this process, the silk is tautly stretched to a frame. The image to be printed is prepared on the silk so that areas not wanted in the design are blocked out; all open areas in the silk will print. The most simple manner of preparing the silk is by using a paper stencil. Other resist materials are glue, lacquer, and special film that is cut and applied to the silk. For backgrounds, a simple placement of strong shapes or a subtle linear image is sufficient if additional work is to be done in another medium. Complex printing would not be appropriate. See *Design on Fabric* by Meda Johnson and Glen Kaufman for additional information on the various methods of silk-screen printing.

The panel on page 127, shows one approach to combining silk-screen printing with stitchery. The background is sheer, off-white dacron, with opaque white ink used in the screened image. Since the design of the print is an arrangement of graceful, circular lines suggesting architectural details, it is not overly prominent. Some of the contrast of the opaque ink over the transparent cloth is difficult to convey in the photograph. Fine embroidery thread is used in the overstitching, which follows the printed lines while adding additional accents and detail.

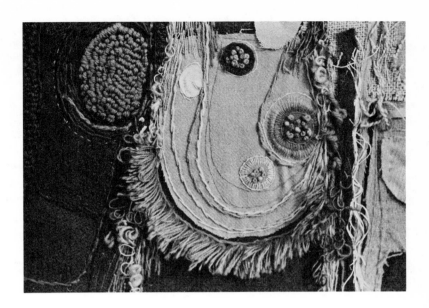

# 18 Hooking Techniques

An effective means of adding a dimensional quality to the textile surface is by utilizing simple methods of hooking and knotting. Although thought of primarily as a method for making rugs, the textural qualities achieved by these techniques are very compatible with many types of stitching and appliqué. Appropriately used, hooking or knotting sections worked into the design add depth by building varying surface heights. These raised areas are in distinct relief from the background.

Hooking is essentially a nonloom rug-making technique. Its simplicity has made it enormously appealing since Colonial times, and even today, many textile artists find ever-increasing possibilities for applying the technique to more expressive purposes. Historically, pieces of woven fabric from discarded clothing were cut into long, narrow strips. When many strips of different colors were collected, they were worked through a sturdy background fabric, forming closely placed rows of loops on the top.

In contemporary work, yarns of all types, as well as precut cloth strips, can be used. The selection of a background material need not

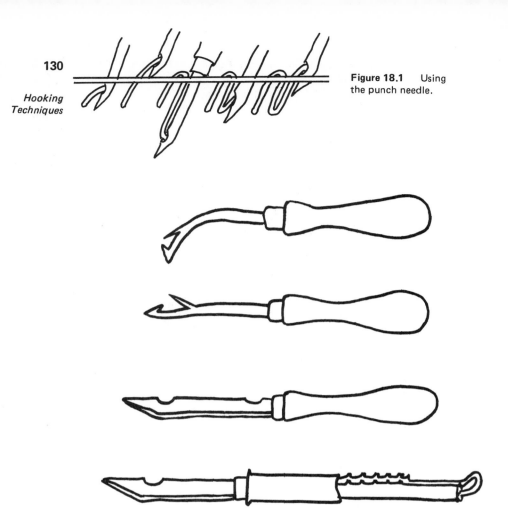

**Figure 18.1**   Using
the punch needle.

**Figure 18.2**   Tools used to form a pile or raised loop surface on
the background fabric. The hand hooks, shown at the top, are
worked on the right side of the cloth; the punch needles, shown
below, are worked from the reverse side.

be limited by a concern for durability when hooking methods are
used in wall hangings and other nonutilitarian pieces. Heavy burlap
and monk's cloth are traditional choices for background fabric; but
many other types of cloth can be used for hooking, as long as the
weave is loose enough for the needle to be pushed through. Medium-
to heavyweight woolens are excellent as ground material for hooking
in selected areas and can relate effectively to additional work in
stitching and appliqué.

Several kinds of tools are available for hooking, including the
punch needle, the crochet-type hand hook, and various semiauto-
matic hand hookers. One of the easiest to use is the punch needle.
With the cloth tacked to a frame, the shape to be hooked is outlined

with chalk on the back side. The needle is worked from the back, with the loops projecting through to the right side, as illustrated in Fig. 18.1. Some needles have a means of adjusting the height of the loops, and these can be used if appropriate.

To insure the evenness of the loops, keep the left hand on the loops, guiding and holding each new loop as it is formed. If an unusually deep loop is wanted, the left hand can draw additional yarn from the needle each time it is inserted. This seems like a tedious process when described, but it is actually very rapid if one is familiar with the use of the tool.

Many kinds of yarn can be used in the punch needle, providing the total thickness is not too great to go through the channel with ease. Several thicknesses and various textures of yarns can be combined. The loops should be worked in rows fairly close together for a solidly filled surface. After hooking is completed, the loops can be left uncut, or cut with a sharply pointed scissors.

The panel on this page shows how small areas of hooking can be used along with stitching and appliqué. The hooked shapes add a complexity to the surface by providing a variation in height. In the circular shapes, the loops are dense and left uncut; the ends of the loops have been clipped in the lines of deeper hooking in the other sections. The background is a heavy wool fabric, with all of the hooking worked in woolen yarns.

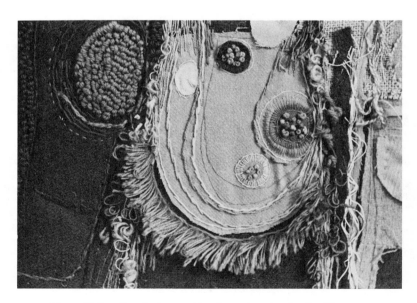

**Figure 18.3**   Detail of a panel by the author showing hooking effects of different types.

Figure 18.4    Inserting the punch needle from the wrong side of the cloth. The line and circular shape on the right show completed areas of hooking from the reverse side.

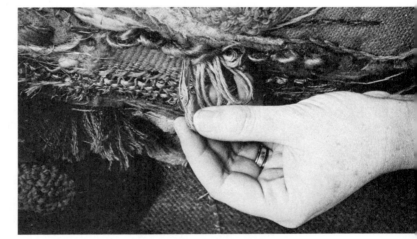

Figure 18.5    The needle is bringing the yarn to the right side of the work. The left hand draws additional yarn from the needle to form a longer loop.

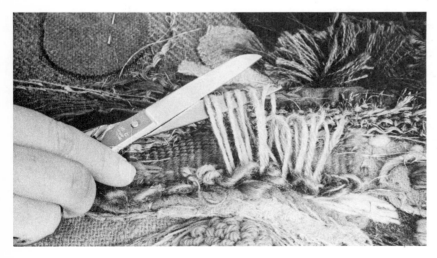

Figure 18.6    Cutting the loops

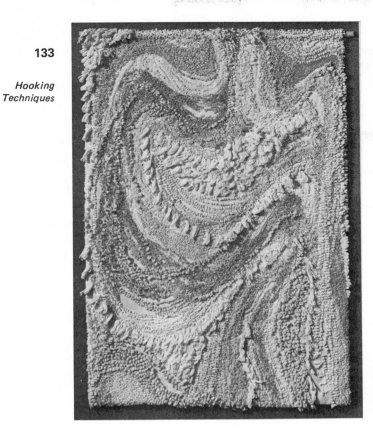

**Figure 18.7** Many different types of yarn, as well as cut strips of cloth, are used in this wall hanging (33" x 48") done completely in the hooking technique by Tsipora Levy.

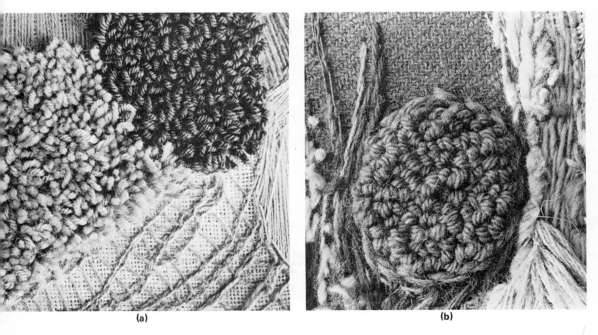

(a)                                                                           (b)

**Figure 18.8**    Detail views of hooking.

Another approach to this technique is seen in the wall hanging on page 133. This piece is done entirely in hooking, with a tremendous range of surface effects achieved by textural variation in the types of yarn used and many changes in the heights of the loops. The crochet-type hand hook was used. This tool is worked from the top; while the left hand holds and guides the yarn on the back side, the hand hook is pushed into the fabric so that it catches the yarn. Then, it is pulled up to the right side, bringing up enough yarn to form the appropriate loop height. This procedure is repeated in curved or straight rows, depending on the design.

The hand hook is excellent for making loops with unusually bulky yarns. Cut strips of cloth can also be hooked with this tool. Learning to use the punch needle and the hand hook is not difficult and certainly well worth the short practice time required until the tools become comfortable to hold and easy to control.

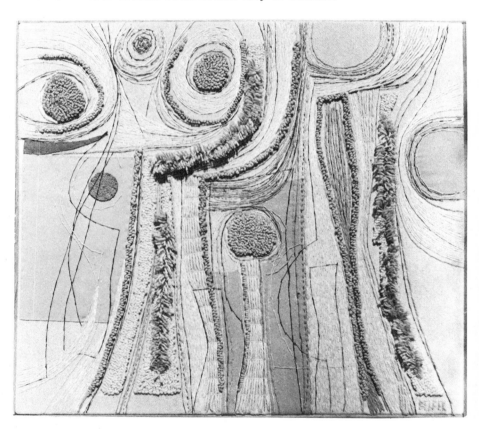

**Figure 18.9**    Hooking in short uncut loops, as well as longer loops that have been cut, are seen in this panel by the author. The stitching and appliqué are in browns, whites, and grays on a beige wool background.

# 19 Forms in Cloth Construction

Using cloth in a sculptural way offers exciting possibilities in the actual building of form. Although full of trial and error adventures for the beginner as well as for the more experienced worker, it is a challenging way of using fabric and open to many innovative approaches.

There is little, historically, that can serve as a guide, so each idea must be developed from the cloth itself. Inspiration can come from ways in which other materials have been used sculpturally for three-dimensional and relief effects. However, it is the intrinsic qualities of fabric and yarn that must be explored and utilized. The way a particular kind of cloth behaves when folded, pleated, crumpled, stretched, or stuffed should be carefully explored. This kind of first-hand observation becomes the most reliable guide.

Many of the techniques previously described can be applied to cloth construction. In addition to stitching and appliqué, stuffing and knotting have also been utilized in the examples illustrated. It is often necessary to incorporate some kind of supporting structure to hold the weight of the cloth or delineate the form. For this, hoops of

135

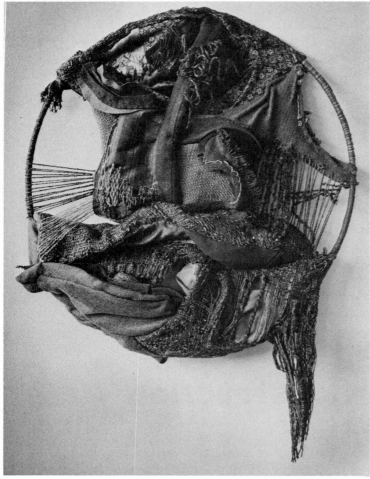

(a)

**Figure 19.1** *Round Landscape*
(30" d.), by Patricia Rogers, is a cloth
construction structured on a metal hoop.
It rotates when suspended.

(b)

**Figure 19.2**    Shaped and stuffed wall hanging, by Bonnie Jerrett,
has fringe effects in both cut cloth and yarn. Background is black
velour.

metal or wood or specially constructed frames are appropriate. Sometimes, the ideal supporting frame can be found in a discarded barrel rim, bicycle wheel, lampshade, or metal grating ... even a woven straw hat can inspire an imaginative idea that can be expressed with yarns and cloth used in a structural way.

The idea can be built solidly on the supporting frame; or open spaces can be left within the work so that light, and sometimes movement, become important considerations. Both of these approaches are combined in *Round Landscape,* on page 138. A heavy metal hoop, about 30 inches in diameter, was used to support the weight of the cloth. Designed with both closed and open areas, both sides are finished so that when the form is suspended, it can be viewed from all sides.

Much of the effectiveness of this work is due to the beautiful colors (greens, yellow-greens, orange, gold, and brown) and the variety of cloth surfaces from shiny to dull. The subtle relief changes in the forms result in a craterlike surface appearance. Many kinds of upholstery cloth scraps are used, put together as appliqué sections with hand sewing. Some areas are left flat, others are treated as multilayers and stuffed. In some parts of the design, masses of threads are pulled out of lengths of fabric, resulting in a fringe effect.

The stitched and stuffed form on page 139 is constructed of black velour, with stitching and appliqué in different kinds of yarns and cloth. A small piece of driftwood has also been incorporated into the design. The back is of the same fabric as the front, with the stuffing added as each of the shapes was stitched. All of the stitching was done by hand.

A strip of the velour cloth, about 5 inches wide, was cut into narrow bands and stitched onto the piece as a heavy fringe. The long fringe was made of many strands of rayon yarn stitched directly to the form and extending down about two feet. The ends of the fringe yarn were dipped in black dye to better relate to the background cloth. This piece needed no frame; it is self-supporting when suspended.

Very different in design, the construction, *Turnabout,* on page 141, shows another approach to using a round support. In this case, the spokes were removed from a discarded bicycle rim which was then covered with natural burlap and used as the frame. The sausagelike stuffed forms were built of bias strips of hand-dyed cotton muslin, stitched around on one side, stuffed with cotton batting and then stitched down on the other side. Additional shapes of burlap and upholstery fabrics were applied to the design with surface stitching; hand hooking was also used in some areas. The form can be turned about freely, since the design elements work effectively when the piece is hung from any point on the rim of the circle.

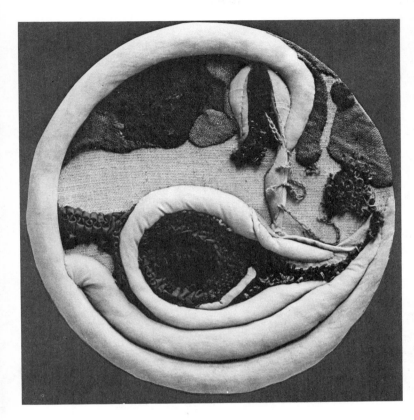

**Figure 19.3** *Turnabout* (26'' d.), by Ruth Bilowus, was built around a discarded bicycle wheel. Appliqué areas and stitching are surrounded by stuffed, curved, tubular forms.

**Figure 19.4** A giant insect, (about 18'' x 28'') was constructed of cloth and decorated with yarns by Charlotte Cippola. Brightly colored stitching covers the velvet body. The wings are built of window screening encased and embroidered with yarns.

**Figure 19.5** An old boiler pipe serves as the base for this knotted and stitched construction, about 36″ high by Patricia Rogers.

**Figure 19.6** Detail shows the smaller metal hoops within the structure for additional support.

**Figure 19.7**    Constructed form in crochet and stitching by Marie
T. Kelly.

**Figure 19.8** *Growth* (50″ x 22″), by the author shows the use of handwoven sections of fabric used as appliqué material integrated with stitching.

**Figure 19.9** In the detail view, the marked texture of the woven cloth is clearly seen, together with the surface stitching and padded areas.

# 20 Soft Objects and Toys

Beautiful objects of cloth are delightful to live with, not only as soft sculpture to be enjoyed visually but as hardy toys that are as much a part of the child's world as the adult's. The three-dimensional figures in cloth are creative excursions into memory, giving form to the myths and legends of childhood. These include storybook and circus figures and, especially, fantastic birds and animals.

Throughout history, birds and animals have been used as motifs on textiles, often as symbols of power or superhuman strength. In ancient literature, animals have been worshipped and assigned tasks no human could perform. Today, the birds and animals that were once feared can be safely observed in zoos and circuses; they are often portrayed as gentle, whimsical creatures.

The examples illustrated here reflect this attitude of playfulness and, sometimes, humor. The velvet peacock is arrogantly displaying his well-stuffed tail, the lines of each feather hand-drawn with dye. The elephant toy has a body of crumpled-up cloth scraps stitched by hand to stay them in place. The head and feet are slightly padded and the ears formed over a fine wire frame. The left ear is rigged to a

143

*Soft Objects
and Toys*

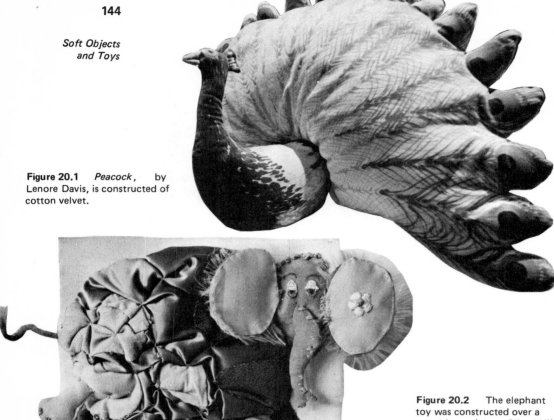

**Figure 20.1** *Peacock*, by Lenore Davis, is constructed of cotton velvet.

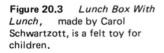

**Figure 20.2** The elephant toy was constructed over a wood frame (about 8″ x 10″) by Ruth Bilowus.

**Figure 20.3** *Lunch Box With Lunch*, made by Carol Schwartzott, is a felt toy for children.

**Figure 20.4** Knotted, stitched, and stuffed doll by Patricia Butler.

**Figure 20.5** Trapeze figures by Susan Hofmeister. The bodies are of cloth, the faces of cutout old photographs.

small, hidden winding device taken from a discarded toy. When the knob is wound, the ear wiggles.

The felt toy, *Lunch Box with Lunch*, encourages a second look at the ordinary things about the house that are used and handled daily. Kitchen tools and food items can become art objects, as well as pleasurable toys, when reformed with cloth. Felt was used to construct this toy, with the hemming and decorative appliqué done with machine stitching. The box is lightly padded with dacron batting; polyester filling is used to stuff the smaller objects. The *Mouse and Cheese*, in the color section, is another part of this series of three-dimensional toy forms.

All of these objects are imaginative ways of using cloth in a sculptural manner. Without being pretentious, they convey the natural qualities of the cloth, even though several techniques are often combined in the same work. The feeling for both the cloth and the structural aspects of the forms is clearly evident. The sophistication of work such as this does not negate the value of its direct appeal and special fascination.

Each individual has within him many kinds of capacities that are seldom fully realized. Creative activities can be diverted in favor of so-called practical pursuits, but the more personal and reflective aspects of one's nature sometimes call out for a means of expression. Yarns and cloth have been used in many ways to make beautiful objects; looking at and reading about these ways can initiate a beginning, encourage further work. These examples, all together, form an atmosphere, an environment of ideas that anyone can find and relate to in his own way. There are no real recipes or rules but many sparks that could prove inspiring.

**Figure 20.6**    A cubist-type construction of stuffed cloth forms about 12″ x 12″ x 12″ in size, by Ruth Bilowus.

# Suppliers

*CLOTH*

*Cottons, woolens, rayons, and synthetic fabrics in various weights; some burlap, felt, and linen; fringes:*
local fabric and drapery shops

*Osnaburg canvas, cotton, and plastic mesh:*
local industrial bag suppliers

*Burlap, variety of colors:*
Bon Bazaar, Inc., 149 Waverly Place, New York, N.Y. 10014

*Felt, variety of colors:*
Central Shippee, 24 West 25th Street, New York, N.Y. 10010

*Textured cottons, unusually wide:*
Homespun House, 9024 Linblade Avenue, Culver City, CA. 90230

*Natural linen:*
Utrecht Linens, 32 Third Avenue, New York, N.Y.

## YARNS

*Wool and synthetic four-ply knitting yarn; cotton embroidery floss, threads, some bulky yarns:*
local department stores, yarn shops

*Natural jute cord, undyed sisal:*
local suppliers of paper and twine

*Selection of twines, cords, and rope:*
local marine supply stores

*Variety of yarns of unusual interest; write for sample cards:*
(by mail order)
Craft Yarns of Rhode Island, Main Street, Harrisville, R.I. 02830
The Fiber Studio, P.O. Box 356, Sudbury, MA. 01776
Greentree Ranch Wools, N. Carter Lake Rd., Loveland, CO. 80537
Lily Mills, Dept. Box 88, Shelby, N.C. 28150

*Handspun Mexican yarn:*
Mexiskeins, Inc., PO Box 1624, Missoula, MT. 59801

*Handspun yarn from Greece:*
Tahki Imports, 836 Palisades Avenue, Teaneck, N.J. 07666

*Yarns—wool, acrylic, rug craft supplies, looms, and weaving supplies:*
Village Weaver Studio, 551 Church Street, Toronto, Canada M4Y2E2
Yarn Depot, 545 Sutter Street, San Francisco, CA. 94102

## ADDITIONAL SUPPLIES

*Trims, braids, laces, buttons, needles:*
local dressmaker and tailor's suppliers

*Needles that cannot be found locally:*
Boye Needle Co., 195 Bonhomme Street, Hackensack, N.J. 07601

*Assortment of decorative beads of wood, glass, plastic, and clay:*
Glasser Bead Co., 49 West 47th Street, New York, N.Y. 10026
Bethlehem Imports, 1169 Cushman Street, San Diego, CA. 92110

*Beads for macramé include wood, glass, and ceramic:*
Gloria's Glass Garden, Box 1990-N, Beverly Hills, CA. 90213

Additional sources of supplies and materials can be found by reviewing advertisements in *Shuttle, Spindle & Dyepot* and *Craft Horizons*.

# Bibliography

## HISTORICAL BACKGROUND

Birrell, Verla. *The Textile Arts.* New York: Harper & Row, 1959.

Bossert, H. T. *Folk Art of Primitive Peoples.* New York: Praeger, 1955.

D'Harcourt, Raoul. *Textiles of Ancient Peru and Their Techniques.* Seattle: University of Washington Press, 1962.

Fel, Edit. *Hungarian Peasant Embroidery.* London: Batsford, 1961.

Jones, Eirwen Mary. *A History of Western Embroidery.* New York: Watson-Guptill, 1969.

Johnstone, Pauline. *Greek Island Embroidery.* London: Tiranti, 1961.

————. *The Byzantine Tradition in Church Embroidery.* Chicago: Argonaut, 1967.

Kassell, Hilda. *Stitches in Time.* New York: Duell, Sloan & Pierce, 1967.

Plath, Ilona, *Decorative Arts of Sweden.* New York: Dover, 1965.

Schuette, Marie. *Pictorial History of Embroidery.* New York: Praeger, 1964.

Slivka, Rose. *Crafts of the Modern World.* New York: Horizon Press, 1968.

Stenton, Sir Frank (ed.). *Bayeux Tapestry.* New York: Phaidon, 1965.

Wheeler, Monroe. *Textiles and Ornaments of India.* New York: Museum of Modern Art, 1966.

Yamanobe, T. *Textiles: Arts and Crafts of Japan.* Rutland, Vt: Tuttle, 1957.

## STITCHING AND APPLIQUÉ

Anders, Nedda. *Appliqué Old and New.* New York: Hearthside Press, 1967.

Bakke, Karen. *The Sewing Machine as a Creative Tool.* Englewood Cliffs, N.J.: Prentice-Hall, Inc., 1976.

Enthoven, Jacqueline. *Stitches of Creative Embroidery.* New York: Van Nostrand Reinhold, 1965.

Frew, Hannah. *Three Dimensional Embroidery.* New York: Van Nostrand Reinhold, 1975.

Foss, Mildred. *Creative Embroidery with Your Sewing Machine.* Englewood Cliffs, N.J.: Prentice-Hall, Inc., 1976.

Howard, Constance. *Inspiration for Embroidery.* Newton Centre, Mass.: Charles T. Branford, 1966.

Karasz, Mariska. *Adventures in Stitches.* New York: Funk and Wagnalls, 1959.

Krevitsky, Nik. *Stitchery: Art and Craft.* New York: Van Nostrand Reinhold, 1966.

LaLiberté, Norman. *Banners and Hangings.* New York: Van Nostrand Reinhold, 1967.

Laury, Jean. *Appliqué Stitchery.* New York: Van Nostrand Reinhold, 1967.

————. *Quilts and Coverlets.* New York: Van Nostrand Reinhold, 1971.

Marein, Shirley. *Stitchery, Needlepoint, Appliqué and Patchwork.* New York: Viking, 1974.

Meilach, Dona. *Soft Sculpture and Other Art Forms.* New York: Crown, 1974.

Murray, Aileen. *Design in Fabric and Thread.* New York: Watson-Guptill, 1969.

Newman, Thelma. *Quilting, Patchwork, Appliqué and Trapunto.* New York: Crown, 1974.

Risley, Christine. *Creative Embroidery.* New York: Watson-Guptill, 1969.

Short, Erian. *Embroidery and Fabric Collage.* New York: Charles Scribner's Sons, 1971.

Springall, Diana. *Canvas Embroidery.* Newton Centre, Mass.: Charles T. Branford, 1969.

Whyte, Katherine. *Design in Embroidery.* Newton Center, Mass.: C. T. Branford, 1969.

Wilcox, Donald. *New Design in Stitchery.* New York: Van Nostrand Reinhold, 1970.

Wilson, Erica. *Crewel Embroidery.* New York: Scribners, 1962.

## RELATED TEXTILE TECHNIQUES

Belfer, Nancy. *Designing in Batik and Tie Dye.* Worcester, Mass.: Davis Publications, 1972 (cloth edition). Englewood Cliffs, N.J.: Prentice-Hall, Inc. (paper edition).

————. *Weaving.* Worcester, Mass.: Davis Publications, 1974.

Brown, Elsa. *Creative Quilting.* New York: Watson-Guptill, 1974.

Chamberlain, Marcia and Candace Crockett. *Beyond Weaving.* New York: Watson-Guptill, 1974.

Christensen, Jo. *The Needlepoint Book.* Englewood Cliffs, N.J.: Prentice-Hall, Inc., 1976.

Ericson, Janet. *Block Printing on Textiles.* New York: Watson-Guptill, 1973.

**152**

Gibbs, Joanifer. *Batik Unlimited*. New York: Watson-Guptill, 1974.

Harvey, Virginia. *Macramé: The Art of Creative Knotting*. New York: Van Nostrand Reinhold, 1967.

Hollander, Annette. *Decorative Papers and Fabrics*. New York: Van Nostrand Reinhold, 1971.

Hoppe, Elizabeth. *Free Weaving on Frame and Loom*. New York: Van Nostrand Reinhold, 1974.

Johnson, Meda and Kaufman, Glen. *Design on Fabric*. New York: Van Nostrand Reinhold, 1967.

Meilach, Donna. *Macramé*. New York: Crown, 1970.

Monk, Kathleen. *Fun with Fabric Printing*. New York: Taplinger, 1969.

Regensteiner, Elsie. *The Art of Weaving*. New York: Van Nostrand Reinhold, 1971.

Robinson, Stuart. *Exploring Fabric Printing*. Newton Centre, Mass.: C. T. Branford, 1970.

Schwalbach, Mathilda. *Screen Process Printing*. New York: Van Nostrand Reinhold, 1970.

Wilson, Jean. *Anyone Can Weave*. New York: Van Nostrand Reinhold, 1967.